W9-BAY-993

TENNIS
for
THINKING
PLAYERS

By Chet Murphy

TENNIS

for

THINKING PLAYERS

By Chet Murphy

2ND EDITION

LEISURE PRESS

A publication of
Leisure Press
P.O. Box 3; West Point, N.Y. 10996

ISBN 0-88011-251-4

First edition: published in 1982.
Second edition: published March, 1985

Front cover photo: Nancy MacGregor of Colorado Springs
Front cover design: Brian Groppe

PHOTO CREDITS:
Cheryl Traendly: 6, 10, 21. 22, 36, 44, 56, 56, 68, 90, 100, 108, 122, 144 and 164

Plus photographs used by permission of **College and Junior Tennis** magazine and photographs by David Cradeur, Janeart, Bob McIntyre and Richard
Zoller.

TABLE OF CONTENTS

Chet Murphy, the author, is shown applying one of the major points of his instruction—hitting with a bent arm so the racket can be made to move along an imaginary target line as it passes through the contact area. Here he is beginning to flatten the arc of his swing by extending his arm as he goes into his follow through (see page 39).

PREFACE

Most knowledgeable observers of the tennis scene agree that the so-called "inner game" is no longer as popular as it once was. Most of us who teach professionally know many players who have tried inner tennis and have given up on it. These players usually offer a simple explanation for their disappointment with it: its main theme— to "watch the ball and let it happen" — mistakenly induced them to minimize the importance of good strokes. As a result, their improvement, if any, was only temporary. Their inadequate strokes with their resulting deficiencies in shots remained apparent despite the "new" theory that we all have built-in good strokes and that we need only to relax on the court and let them emerge naturally. Many of these players admit that they are not only playing badly because of experimenting with inner tennis techniques, but that they are losing to players they had often beaten earlier.

No wonder that emphasis in teaching and learning the game is still on the basics. Most knowledgeable and experienced teachers still stress stroke practice in which learners consciously think about developing an efficient and effective way to hit the ball.

If you've had the experience I've described above, if you've discovered that there must be more to learning to play well than simply relaxing and swinging naturally, this book is for you. But it is also intended for readers who are not familiar with inner tennis. Regardless of whether you are self-taught or were taught by a teacher or a "pro," if you appreciate the importance of good strokes and if you accept the need for practice to develop your strokes, there is something here for you.

A large majority of skilled players learned to play this way, by thinking of how to play. Few of them believe they were born with good strokes. Rather, they are proud to have developed their strokes through many hours of practice, and they admit to continuing to fine-tune and hone their strokes through additional practice.

The history and literature of the game is replete with incidents of even world-class players taking time off from tournament play to work on certain parts of their games. For example, we read that both Bill Tilden and Don Budge spent winter months revamping their forehands. I remember, too, that Jack Kramer spent an equal amount of time developing his serve-and-volley techniques. As you would expect, this kind of dedication extends to today's crop of players.

We know, for example, that Bjorn Borg gave himself a two-week practice period before one of his five successful Wimbledon tournaments during which time he worked almost exclusively on his serve. Since that time Borg has learned to serve his share of aces. And, among the women, both Chris Evert and Andrea Jaeger are known to have improved their volleys in off-season practice sessions designed specifically for that purpose. They considered this necessary despite being ranked among the five best women players in the world.

Surely if there were an easier way to develop strokes, a natural way, players of this caliber would know of it and would use it. Instead, we see that even they have to revert to the same long-established methods the rest of us must go through—thoughtful practice. No indeed, good strokes don't just happen; they have to be learned, which explains the purpose of this book.

Here in this book I will describe what you can and should think about during practice and during play-for-practice to develop your strokes. But as a preliminary to that I will describe how your nervous system—your muscles, sense organs and brain—functions during physical activity. I'll also describe what to think about during a match, explaining how you might train yourself to reduce tension and pressure that inhibits successful performance. And, lastly, I'll discuss several points of strategy and tactics you can learn to use effectively in various play situations.

Since strokes are the tools you use to apply tactics and strategy, I'll describe several points of form to consider during stroke practice. I'll present several simple facts of physics, (of the branch of physics known as biomechanics), that will help you understand how to stroke the ball efficiently while not totally changing your present strokes.

My instruction here is flexible. I don't stress one specific stroke pattern, one particular "look," so to speak, and ask all readers to conform to it. Rather, I suggest that you simply adjust your present strokes to put them in accord with selected mechanical principles, with your own individual abilities and your own personal preferences. To promote such freedom of choice, I offer options in points of form and I suggest that you experiment with these options to determine which work best for you.

You see, then, that I'm suggesting you think about your strokes rather than to simply go through the motions of stroking while hoping for the best. I'm also suggesting that you think about tactics and strategy both before a match and during play so you can put those strokes to best use. Hence the title of this book: Tennis For Thinking Players.

If you're doubtful that thinking during play is important, consider what two of the world's best players say about the matter. Guillermo Vilas (winner over Jimmy Connors in the 1977 U.S. Open at Forest Hills) says his climb to the top was due in large part to his increasing ability to think during the heat of battle. And Virginia Wade, 1977

Wimbledon champion, says she learned only a few years before that a tennis match is an intellectual contest as well as a physical one, and that she has enjoyed the game more and has played better as a result.

Wade gives still another example of the importance of thinking during play. After beating Rosie Casals for the first time in three tries, she said, "I played much better tonight. The big difference was my concentration. Even if you're not playing well, you should be able to think your way out."

As we consider Wade's remarks we must acknowledge that stroking a tennis ball is more a physical act than a mental exercise. So physical ability is essential for good play. We must also recognize that a tennis match is more an athletic contest than an art form. So good strokes alone do not win matches. And so, like Wade, we must conclude that our game is a combination of brain and brawn, in which the mind and body interact, each affecting the other.

It was with this combination, this interaction in mind, that I established the purpose of this book: to help you by showing how to integrate—or, if you prefer, to synthesize—the physical and mental aspects of play. My intention is to help you learn to use your mind and your racket more effectively in play. In other words, to help you become a thinking player.

Bjorn Borg has said that he often has a headache from thinking so hard during his long matches. Here he could be thinking of what he intends to do, namely, pull the racket up off the back of the ball.

CHAPTER 1

PLAY WHILE YOU THINK

OOOOOOOOOOOOOOOOOOOOOOOOOOOOOOOOO

ANALYZE YOUR MISSES

Surely at times during serious play, you have missed easy shots that you normally make. Afterward, when you recall those misses and search for reasons for them, you often decide that you were either too relaxed or too tense. Typically, in these first instances, players say, "My mind wandered," or, "I got careless." For the second group of misses, we hear, "God, I was afraid to hit it," or, the most descriptive expression of all, "I choked."

To avoid your misunderstanding both the purpose and the content of this book, let me state how I feel about these kinds of analyses. For over thirty years I have seen situations like these occur. Now, looking back at them from my vantage point of an experienced player, teacher and coach, I conclude that many players mistakenly attribute most of their easy misses to mental pressure and tension. Undoubtedly, many misses do occur for that reason. But it is just as likely that a particular missed shot could be the result of bad physical performance not directly caused by mental factors.

For example, a player may miss an easy backhand volley because the elbow is raised or because the grip is loose or because the racket is pulled away from the ball, all of which may be done inadvertently for reasons we are not able to explain.

We see this occur in other sports, too. Why, for example, does Jack Nicklaus shoot a 69 one day and a 74 on the next round even when practicing on the same course? Why doesn't Reggie Jackson hit every pitch out of the park during batting practice when the pitcher is throwing nicely over home plate? And why does Ray Guy punt only 40 yards on one kick and 60 yards on the next one during his pre-game practice when there is no opposition to his kicking? We can hardly say they choke on every bad shot or bad swing or bad kick while practicing.

There must be some other reason, a reason I hope to explain to your satisfaction in the remainder of this chapter. And in the remainder of this book I hope to be able to help you minimize the number of bad shots you make, whatever the reason for your making them.

I've been aware of this overemphasis on mental pressure as an explanation for errors ever since an incident occurred at my club years ago. While playing in a social doubles match with three good friends I happened to be serving on match point. Lo and behold, I served a double fault, my first of the match, the second ball sailing too long and beyond the service court. One of the opponents immediately called "choke," in jest (I hope) but also to explain why he thought I missed the shot. But I didn't choke. I sometimes do, as does everyone. But, not on this occasion, in this friendly, unimportant match. I tried one of my best shots, a medium-paced spin serve, placed deep to the backhand and followed by a rush to the net. That shot and those tactics usually work for me at that level of competition.

So how do I explain my miss? I simply placed my racket inaccurately on the ball, hitting under it too much. But I swung with the same unpressured stroke I had used for the entire match.

While trying to understand my miss, and those of Nicklaus, Jackson, and Guy as well, we have to conclude that there is something going on between—and in—the minds and bodies of performers that we can not fully explain. It is something that enables them to swing or to hit or to kick well on one attempt and yet to do it less effectively on the next attempt—even when not performing under pressure.

But for the better players, their technique, their form, is good enough often enough to make them more consistent long-range performers than the rest of us.

None of them are perfect. The best of them miss more often than they like, even those who are totally dedicated to their games.

It may help you understand how this is possible and even likely if we consider what happens physically during a tennis stroke. Specifically, let's consider my serve. It is a typical, orthodox swing, with no unnecessary mannerisms that could possibly interfere with good form. And so by describing it, I will also be describing the broad general pattern of most good servers.

From the ready posture I move my arm at the shoulder to swing my racket into a downward arc past my right knee. At the low point of the arc I raise my arm behind me to raise the racket. As it points toward the top of the rear fence I turn my body counterclockwise and bend my arm at the elbow, letting the racket drop into the backscratching position. When it is down as far as I can get it, I pull it up toward the ball by straightening my arm and flexing my wrist. Simultaneously I rotate my upper arm and pronate my forearm to open the racket face for contact.

Though this description of the swing makes it sound rather disjointed, the arm can be made to function rather smoothly in a crack-the-whip manner. But with so much happening during a serve, much can go wrong. The joint movements must be applied in sequence with each one coming in at the peak of the previous one. If one follows too late after the preceding one, the momentum from the preceding one will be lost. If a force is applied too soon, the total effect of two consecutive forces will be reduced. In other words, timing must be good.

But even while applying forces in the proper sequence and with good timing, I must control my racket speed and direction so that I can finally place it properly on the ball. In the case of the double-fault mentioned earlier, I can only conclude that I inadvertently placed my racket too low on the ball while swinging upward to apply spin. The combination of low contact point and upward swing sent the ball into a higher trajectory than I had intended. The result was the long serve, the double fault.

When we consider that the tolerance for error as regards the position of the racket on the ball is minimal (often as little as 3 degrees), we can understand why misses often occur. In addition, since such precise placement of implements against balls is required in other sports, we can also understand misses there.

There are other critical factors that explain why even superstars hit into the net or strike out or miss an easy shot. Some body joints permit their adjacent limbs to move rather freely in several directions. At the shoulder, for example, the arm may be raised or lowered, and it may be moved forward or backward. These moves may be combined in any manner to swing the arm diagonally in its socket. And, finally, the arm may be rotated either clockwise or counterclockwise even while making any of the other moves.

Similar freedom of movement is possible at the hip joint allowing the leg to be moved in several planes and in several directions. At the elbow and knee joints, movement is restricted somewhat and the lower arm and leg do not move as freely nor in as many directions. At the wrist and ankle joints, however, extensive freedom is again permitted. With so much movement possible, some control is necessary. Muscles are the controlling force and these are brought into action by the athlete when he/she decides to swing or to kick or to lift or to lower.

In sports, movements of the limbs are not naturally made as solid, rigid, one-piece swings. Instead, there is a tendency for some looseness between joints of the limbs, a kind of "slack," that makes the limb segments function like links in a chain. Movement at a close-in joint, or link, is likely to affect the positions and movements of segments that are farther out from that joint. You can imagine, therefore, what precise muscular control is necessary to guide these movements, to control the force of them, to permit only those that are wanted and to restrict unnecessary ones, and to keep the limb segments in proper alignment. Skilled performers make these adjustments more accurately than others; but not every time. They miss shots, too, often for the same reason that I served the double fault described earlier: miscalculation.

You might think this unlikely, considering the many hours they spend in practice and in play. You might think they would be able to groove their swings to make them alike, time after time. They can't, however. Nor would grooving help much, for the reason that no two play situations are exactly alike.

For example, a particular service swing may appear to be like any other one because of apparent similarities in conditions. But, are those conditions similar? Not really. With the variety of motions in a swing, it's impossible for anyone to reproduce them in the same manner, in the same intervals of time, and with the same amount of force. If one motion differs from that same motion in previous serves, other motions in that newer serve will differ as well. Specifically, if the body weight is shifted sooner or later it will affect the timing of the toss and will alter the synchronization between the toss and the swing, requiring adjustment in body action, etc. With so much happening, it's remarkable that a server can manage enough control to make a good serve even occasionally. Yet, through practice, most players learn to adjust those variables in order to control them sufficiently.

You must develop skill at controlling these and similar movements at other joints if you are to perform accurately. Though you may not be blessed with an innate ability to do so, with sufficient practice you can almost certainly learn to make these moves with better timing and with more accuracy than you now do. You may learn how to reduce interference of one movement to another and how to damp out extraneous motion so that only what needs to be done is done. In this way, mannerisms do not become a part of—or worse still, interfere with—good form.

THINK ABOUT YOUR FORM

Good form, the ability to stroke efficiently and effectively, doesn't just come naturally. There is more to learning to play well than simply "letting it happen," despite some recent popularity of that so-called inner-game theory of learning. Good form requires time on the practice court and in match play. It requires energy to make that practice and play beneficial. And it requires mental effort—conscious thought— to direct your body into the many positions and postures that eventually result in good strokes.

Admittedly, after you have built efficient strokes, you'll not have to do a lot of heavy thinking to produce them in play. But, in the process of building strokes, it will be to your advantage to know what you're supposed to do and to recognize what you've done. To do this, you'll have to *think* about your strokes as you practice them. To say it more directly—to learn to play, you have to think about how to play.

To explain how thinking helps in learning a physical act, let me tell you about teaching my young son how to drive a car. He and I were working together in a car with a standard gear shift mechanism: "a stick shift," as he calls it. As do most learners, in his initial attempts he had trouble learning to shift smoothly while he was also trying to control the moving car. He had seen me shift properly time and time again, so he knew what he was supposed to do. Yet he couldn't automatically duplicate my moves. Only when he put his mind specifically to that task, to moving the lever first to the left and down, then to the right and up, etc., was he able to move the car ahead without jerking us out of our seats. Only after several hours of practice and a great deal of imaginary shifting, was he able to shift subconsciously while his mind was on the road and on traffic.

Now you may be wondering what this example of learning to drive has to do with our problems of hitting a tennis ball. I suggest that the process of learning to hit is similar. And again, I draw from my own experience to illustrate.

Recently at my club a woman player came to me and asked for two tune-up lessons before a match she and her husband were to play against another couple. These two teams had played several times before, but always as a social event. In each situation, this woman had trouble returning the opposing man's high-bouncing serve. Now the up-coming match was to be a serious one, a semi-final match in our club tournament, so she wanted to work especially on handling that kind of serve.

In our first lesson I noticed immediately that she had what I call a "droopy backswing." On the forehand she let her racket dip as low as her knees as she drew it back. With the racket down that low, she had trouble raising it properly to swing efficiently at shoulder-high balls. Standing alongside her, I explained this to her and demonstrated how she could adjust the height of her backswing to the height of the bouncing ball. I suggested that she grip her racket more firmly as she started each swing and that she raise her arm at the shoulder to move her racket back from the waiting position.

She learned to do that in a few minutes, and so I began to serve to her to let her apply the new method against the moving ball. As I served ball after ball to her forehand—a high-bouncing serve to her forehand—I prodded her to plan to move her racket up and back as she saw the ball leave my racket. She made several corrected swings, but every now and then I would see her old, droopy swing. Each time I did, I reminded her, from my position across the net, to start her racket up. For this I coined the phrase, "the first move is up." I asked her to think about it and to plan to do it that way each time I prepared to serve to her. Soon she was making the better swing every time. And with it, she was able to place most of her shots at my feet as I ran forward to volley her returns. Naturally, the lesson ended happily.

In our second lesson we practiced in the same way except that I then had less explaining to do. She already knew what to do; it was just a matter of her forming the habit of doing it. And so we got into action sooner and we made progress sooner. Before the lesson was over, she had modified her old droopy swing to the more efficient one I had shown her. Two days later during that important match she had pointed for, her new stroke stood up remarkably and she was elated with the results.

You are probably now aware of the main theme of this book: I hope to encourage you to think while on the tennis court, both during practice and in play. I believe that many of the so-called inner problems such as "choking," "clutching," nervousness, lack of confidence, and fear of missing are caused by outer faults. Faulty judgment and timing, faulty movement and position, and faulty strokes—these cause misses. And so practice—and conscious thought during practice—are necessary to avoid such faults and to correct them. As you do correct them, you will gain confidence in your ability. Only then will that confidence carry over into serious play.

Surely you will agree that if you frequently miss a particular shot in practice because of faulty form (which is usually the cause because here you are not in a stressful situation), there is no reason to expect to be able to make that shot consistently in a match. Don't you also agree that the mental tension you feel is really caused by your fear of missing, which you almost expect to do because you miss so frequently in practice?

I have had this thesis—that inner problems are caused by outer faults—reinforced only recently by an incident that occurred in my school work. An advanced student of mine named Randy asked me to watch him and his partner play a semi-final match in our school doubles tournament. They expected to win and they wanted my coaching afterward for the expected final match to come later. Unfortunately, there was no final for them; they lost the semi-final match that I watched.

In that match Randy played well enough. His partner's weak serves were the reason for their loss. And his weak serving was caused by a grip problem; he used a Western grip. With his hand placed close to the bottom plane of the handle he could not apply sufficient spin to serve effectively. Instead, he served a flat ball even on his second serve. Naturally, he had to hit that ball easily enough for gravity to drag it down into the service court. Just as naturally, the opponents regularly moved forward of their baselines and attacked those weak second serves.

This diagnosis was easy enough for me and Randy to make in our post-match discussion. But his partner did not accept our opinions. He didn't agree that his serve was bad mechanically. Instead, he blamed his poor serving on his mental state, claiming that he "was not at one with the situation, was not in harmony with it," to put it in his exact words. Surely you can imagine why the situation was not harmonious to the server, and to poor Randy who had to defend his net position against aggressive service returns made against his partner's weak serves. It would be easy enough for anyone to be "out of sync" with that tactical situation, don't you agree?

You may not know that the expressions used to describe the hoped-for state of mind, "being at one with" and "in harmony with a situation," are derived from the meditative approach to life espoused by Far Eastern mystics. With the increased popularity of this philosophy in this country, many tennis players (among them, Randy's partner) mistakenly overlook the good old-fashioned way to success: lots of practice. Instead, they hope for some mysterious alchemy of the mind to occur that will in some magical way suddenly give them good strokes and winning shots.

Not likely, I say. To reinforce this point allow me to resurrect a long-buried anecdote that bears directly on the topic. A music student, new and alone in New York, and standing at a corner with violin case in hand asks a passerby, "Please, how do I get to Carnegie Hall?" The answer, as succinct and as appropriate as could be, "Practice."

As it was for our street-walking musician, so it is for you. The best way to attain your goals in tennis, whether they be to win regional titles or club championships or simply to beat your neighbors, is through practice, a great deal of practice, followed by competition, a great deal of competition. And so I plan to tell you what to practice and how to practice. I also plan to tell you how you can use, in serious match play, the strokes and tactics you learn in practice.

But while doing so, I'll not suggest that you change your strokes, or any one stroke, completely. Instead, I hope to encourage you to analyze your strokes and perhaps to increase your knowledge of the mechanics of stroking so you can learn to hit the ball better while still maintaining the broad picture, the total look, of your strokes.

This plan is consistent with my often stated policy of offering flexible tennis instruction. Here I will not make dogmatic assertions that any one method of stroking is better than any other. We see too many good players make too many different things work to permit us, you as a player and me as a teacher, to have such a narrow attitude about how best to hit the ball. Instead, we have to conclude that among the varieties of styles and techniques we see, several are worth trying. And I suggest that this is best done in practice during which you experiment to discover what works best for you. I state strongly that it is in practice that you can start to become a thinking player.

The importance of practice is seldom minimized among serious tournament players. But it often is among inexperienced learners, especially those who look to inner tennis for the quick and easy way to become a better player.

Perhaps we should not be surprised that this mistake occurs. Many of the current tennis writers, particularly those dealing with the mental aspects of the game, overlook the importance of practice. Usually when they use the word at all it is to tell their readers to practice controlling their minds, to practice controlling their mental states, their levels of anxiety, so to speak. Not much is said about practicing strokes.

And, surprisingly, other authors also neglect the importance of practice even while they warn their readers of too much psychology. In one popular journal, the author prompts his readers to remember that everything that happens in the game is not psychological: "Your game may be impaired by fatigue, overeating, accident, or just plain bad luck."

True enough, I say, but faulty strokes and tactics may also impair your game. And the best way to improve these is to work on them in practice as well as in play. After all, hitting a tennis ball is a motor skill, not a mental exercise. And as is done for all motor skills, muscles must be set to work to move bones around joints. And muscles are subject to training, which brings us back to practice. I am not suggesting that all points of form in tennis require prolonged practice. True, some very good players have learned much of what they do in tennis by the straightforward process of trial-and-error. But trial-and-error is not the most efficient way to learn anything.

Certainly, one can learn to play tennis without instruction. But among the many players who learned through the "natural" method, there are several who remain poor players because of inefficient and ineffective habits developed in the natural process. For many of them, technical instructions would have helped avoid faulty habits, faulty stroke patterns, and faulty tactics. Technical instructions that required conscious thought applied to strokes and tactics could have made the difference between playing badly and playing well, between winning and losing, between enjoyment and discouragement. This is the teacher's role: to facilitate learning, to make it easier, more efficient.

If you are still doubtful that thinking can have these effects on tennis strokes, consider what Martina Navratilova said when asked to explain her streak of good serving during a tournament. She said she had worked on that aspect of her game during the previous week while she was conducting clinics. "I was telling all those ladies how to hit their serves," she said, "and I was getting more and more technical. That started me thinking about my own serve, and I think it helped."

Let us consider what probably happened in her lessons. Surely she was not able to pay conscious attention to several details in any one of her own serves. That would have been impossible, and an attempt to have done so would have disrupted the smooth timing and sequence that make her serve so effective. More likely she was thinking about various separate parts of the serve on any particular swing.

Though she knew how to make the total swing, she had to focus on some precise cues to guide the actions of her students. Perhaps she traced the racket's path for them, or showed them how to toss, or when to shift the weight, or how to set the racket at impact. Whatever her cues, she expected each student to focus on them and on the movements indicated by them.

Her own improvement probably resulted from a "carry-over" effect. For example, when she was explaining how to brush up on the ball for topspin she probably demonstrated that motion several times. And to make it obvious, she probably exaggerated it in her own swing, applying more force than previously. Her well-trained body then was able to assimilate that more forceful motion into her total swing, making it more efficient. The result was, in her own judgment, an improved serve.

Having used examples from other sports as well as from tennis to explain the reasons for my anti-inner game attitude, let me now relate a little-known humorous anecdote that will help set an even firmer course for the discussion that follows in the remainder of this book.

Two ministers, good friends and heavy smokers, wondered about the propriety of that habit for men of the cloth. For peace of mind they decided to call their respective superiors for an opinion on the matter. One asked if he might smoke while praying. "Heavens no," he was told. "That would be terribly distracting." The other asked his superior if he could pray while he was smoking. "My lord, yes," was the reply. "Pray at every opportunity."

Now, this subtle difference between smoking while praying and praying while smoking is comparable to the difference between thinking while playing tennis and playing while thinking. I suggest that we learn strokes best by thinking about them. Then, after having learned them, we use them rather subconsciously (in fast play, at least) while we are thinking of the developing pattern of play and of how we can control that pattern.

In the first instance we think while stroking. We may have to think about the position of an arm or leg, about the setting of the racket face, about the plane of the swing, and about the amount of force to apply it. We think about what we are doing.

In the second instance we apply strokes naturally to whatever play situations develop. Our minds are then free to determine which shots to anticipate from our opponent, which tactics of our own to apply, and which strokes to use to make those tactics work. In other words, we play while we are thinking. We think about what we intend to do.

Surely you can see now that the main theme of this book is to encourage you to think your way to better tennis. I hope you will agree, then, that a logical topic for us to consider is the central nervous system—the brain and spinal cord—in which thoughts originate and through which thoughts are converted into action. I discuss this in the chapter that follows.

SUMMARY. The human body is a complicated machine. But most of your moves in tennis are—or can be—under your control. You can direct your body into certain positions and postures, and you can move your limbs as you wish and when you wish. In practice, through experience and experiments, you can learn the moves, positions, and postures that are likely to enable you to make effective shots. This kind of practice can start you to becoming a thinking player.

Billie Jean King, shown hitting defensively from the baseline, says you need to think in order to develop the good strokes that will enable you to make good shots. If you're not thinking, she says, forget it. (Photo by Cheryl A. Traendly)

CHAPTER **2**

TRUST YOUR BODY

OOOOOOOOOOOOOOOOOOOOOOOOOOOOOOOOOOO

We who teach tennis would like to feel that we know exactly what goes on in the minds of our students as we work with them. Until more evidence is gathered from scientific research and from observation, however, we have to admit that we still have much to learn in this area. We can't adequately explain the many changes we see occurring in our students as they develop in the game. But changes are obvious, and in the absence of a better explanation, we can only conclude that they result from changes in their nervous systems.

In one commonly accepted explanation of how learning occurs, the nervous system—the brain and the spinal cord—is made analogous to an electronic computer. Movement and learning in sports are explained in terms of impulses being transmitted via the spinal cord to and from the muscles and the brain. My thirty years of teaching leads me to conclude that much skill learning does indeed take place in this way, and so much of what I say here, and much of what I do when I teach, is based on this theory.

Your brain acts as a command center. It processes data sent to it (in the form of electrical impulses) from your sense organs and from sensory nerve endings in your muscles and around your joints. It may then make a decision to act. If it does, it sends impulses of its own to selected muscles, "triggering" them into action.

In a match, for example, you may *see* your opponent hit a high ball, in which case your brain orders you to move back to get a playable bounce. Or you *hear* the sound of solid impact between the racket and the ball so your brain tells you to expect a fast shot and perhaps a skiddy bounce. At another time you may *sense* your location in the court and may *feel* yourself bending and stretching for a wide, low ball. Here, you are told to exert yourself and to hurry back into position. In all these cases, your brain responds to input from your senses.

But that input, those impulses, may pass through various levels of your spinal cord before reaching the final level of conscious thought in your brain. Yet at any level in the spinal cord an impulse may be diverted from its course to the brain and be routed instead directly to your muscles. In this case, the movement of those muscles is done without any conscious thought on your part.

Perhaps the best example of this in tennis occurs during the volley practice routine known as "reflex volleying." Here, two players volley at each other from close range, trying to hit hard enough to cause each other to miss. Neither player has time to think of what to do or of what he or she is doing. Instead, all moves are made automatically.

When we see this being done or when we do it ourselves, we recognize that much skillful movement goes on below the level of conscious awareness. We have to conclude then that there are various levels of consciousness, ranging from complete unawareness (as in the knee-jerk reflex), to semi-attention, to deep conscious thought. And we perform in sports, just as we do in our everyday routines of life, in varying states of consciousness.

For example, you act at various levels of consciousness when you and a companion walk along a sidewalk. You may be discussing a profound subject and your mind may be fully occupied by it. As you walk and talk you are not fully aware of hazards on the sidewalk, though you manage somehow to avoid them. Your evasive moves, slight changes of direction and slight changes of speed, perhaps, are largely automatic. But suddenly a skateboarder comes zooming along causing people to jump out of his way. The speed and the frightened expressions of other walkers make a vivid impression on you, causing you to suddenly stop talking and to put your attention to reaching a safe location. Plainly, you handled the problems with different levels of attention.

But getting back to tennis, the ability to make the "reflex" moves described in the volley drill doesn't just develop naturally. They, and all the other strokes of the game, must first be *learned*. And that's another process.

SHAPE YOUR STROKES

In the early stages of learning a stroke, many moves are made consciously. For these the brain is involved. Let's assume, for example, that you decide to make a particular kind of forehand swing— one with a circular backswing. In a sense, your brain commands your body into action. In this process your brain thinks of movement, not muscles. It may give a general command such as "bend the arm to raise the racket" rather than a specific command to certain muscles to contract with x amount of force. Later, after learning occurs, the command may be simply to "make a forehand."

I'm not suggesting that you think about all the moves at one time during a stroke. Too much happens too quickly to permit you to do that. But you can work on different parts of your strokes in sequence, emphasizing first one part, then another, and you can learn those parts that way. This procedure by which you build your stroke piece meal is called "shaping" and is generally accepted by learning specialists as an effective procedure.

Though you are probably not a beginner in the game (beginners are not likely to be reading this kind of book), let us pretend for the moment that you are. In forehand stroke practice you may first concentrate on your backswing. At this time, a good teacher would reinforce (praise you) for almost any kind of swing you make. But, to avoid having to approve ridiculously inadequate swings, the teacher would probably use some kind of guidance, a gimmick or a gadget like those I describe in a later chapter, to get you to swing more properly. Gradually, he or she would become more demanding and would commend and praise you only for swings that were very much like the intended final form.

Having reached that stage, your teacher and you may now best concentrate on the next related part of your swing, the forward swing. Here the learning procedure would be similar: approval first even for swings that only vaguely resemble the hoped for final product, and gradually more strict compliance to the teacher's model. When you work on specific parts of your strokes this way, repeating them over and over again, they can be built in to your strokes. Finally, after much practice you may learn to coordinate and to combine the parts of your strokes to make a smooth, efficient and effective whole stroke.

Even when practicing without the help of a teacher you can shape your strokes in a similar way. You have instant feedback every time you hit the ball: your shot was either good or bad, either in or out (possibly even into the net). Naturally, you should try to change your stroke after a miss and should try to repeat it after a good shot. In the next chapter I'll explain what happens physically to cause misses, and with that information you will know what corrections to make.

This suggestion that you evaluate your shots is in opposition to inner-game theory which suggests that you should not be self-judgmental. Inner-game enthusiasts would have you swing away time after time almost as if not caring whether your shots are in or out, while not consciously doing anything about your swings. Somehow, in some mystical way, your shots are supposed to become more accurate.

I saw a perfect demonstration of the deficiencies in this method recently at my own community's public courts where several young instructors conduct lessons for boys and girls.

While waiting for an open court, my playing partner and I were able to watch one of the instructors giving a lesson to two teen-age girls. For almost an hour we saw him feed balls to the girls while offering only two bits of instruction. He told them to watch the ball, and to use a bounce-hit routine. His words were as simple and as concise as that: "watch the ball; bounce hit." Nothing, absolutely nothing more! I recognized these as two main concepts in inner-game theory.

But, try as they might, the girls couldn't hit accurately. In fact, they hit several balls over a fence and into an adjoining court even though the instructor fed what should have been easy-to-handle balls.

Realizing that they weren't doing well, both girls often asked for more instruction, and for an explanation of why they were hitting so

READINESS: Two good examples, one by the player, the other by the linesman, of mental and physical alertness. These players know that mental readiness is usually a concomitant of physical readiness.

wildly. The instructor offered no further advice presumably because he believed that corrections would occur automatically without any conscious thought or direction by the players. Truly, after almost an hour's lesson, only a few balls were hit accurately into the court and many were still sailing over the side fences.

As the lesson ended the girls moved close to us where their bicycles were chained to the fence. While arranging their gear and preparing to mount their bikes, one girl said in a dispirited tone, "Gosh, what can we say to Dad when he asks what we learned today?" Her partner was equally discouraged, obviously, since her reply was a simple, "Really!" If you understand teen-age vernacular, you recognize that as synonymous for "You're so right," or "Isn't that the truth."

Plainly, both girls were displeased with the lesson. I contend that they had good reason for feeling so. They had made no progress (or very little, if any) toward building satisfactory strokes. And worse still, they knew nothing of what to do in future practice. These girls would have improved their shots more quickly had they been given some more appropriate instruction and had they been coached to make some deliberate physical change in their swings. I've seen this method work hundreds of times for hundreds of students. It will probably work best for you as well.

During practice by which you change or shape your strokes, your mind should be on your stroke. It should be on some positive move that is part of that stroke. I'll say more about this later when I talk about cues and anti-choke devices. But, for now let me say again that you should be thinking fully about your strokes during practice so you don't have to concentrate fully on them during play.

UNDERSTAND YOUR BODY

I may appear to be contradicting myself when I suggest that you first think consciously of making a stroke and that later you think less about it. But it may help you undrstand how this is possible if I desribe in more detail some aspects of the body's marvelous communication system.

We all have within us, in ligaments and in tendons, in certain organs and at certain joints, a network of special sense organs called proprioceptors. These special organs enable us to keep track of our body segments, telling us where they are in relation to the environment and in relation to each other. They tell us what our bodies are doing, which movements are occurring at which joints, with which force and at which range. They tell us which muscles to contract and which to relax for any particular motion. And they often do this by bypassing our command center, the brain. As a result, we are able to act at low levels of consciousness.

The points of good form shown here don't just develop naturally. Instead, you have to practice to prepare this well and to have such good posture and weight control. And you're likely to have to apply a great deal of conscious thought during that practice.

These all add up to a kind of sixth sense (often called kinesthetic sense, but here let's call it muscle sense) that enables us to make the smoothly coordinated movements we are capable of making without thinking. It is likely that superior athletes are better able to read the signals being transmitted by their sensors than the rest of us can read ours. It's likely, too, that they can more accurately make the adjustments indicated by the signals than can we, possibly because they are more sensitive at their proprioceptors. Nevertheless, you too are capable of combining conscious decision-making with sub-conscious action, regardless of your level of play.

In a match, for example, you find yourself in a particular play situation. You become aware of your location in your court and of your opponent's location. You recognize the kind of shot he or she is making and you assess your potential for reaching that shot. And you may plan your return shot. In other words, you survey the situation and analyze it logically. You then make a decision to act.

At this point your proprioceptors may take over. They send messages from your muscles and/or your joints, controlling and directing your orientation in space. They give you a sense of feel, or touch, making you aware of such things as where your racket is, how much your elbow is bent, how much your shoulders have turned, how big a step you've taken and other details that are part of a stroke. They also constantly monitor your moves, enabling you to guide them and to control them, to keep your body segments in alignment or to place them properly out of alignment when suitable. They tell you which muscles to contract and which to relax, what to correct and how to do it. You respond by swinging slower or faster, higher or lower, longer or shorter to achieve your purpose.

During this time you may not be aware of what you are doing except to know that you are responding to a general directive from your command center. But you are not likely to make that swing accurately and efficiently unless you have first learned how to make it through conscious thought in practice.

To explain how this occurs during match play, let me describe an experiment I've conducted several times with some of my better college players. I've often arranged for any two of them to play each other while I watched. They were told to play seriously, to the best of their ability, with the understanding that I, as coach, could interrupt play at any time to discuss the match. In accordance with that agreement, I frequently stopped play *after a crucial point* to ask them what they were thinking of during the point. I recorded their replies so I could write about them accurately here. Read what some of them said.

"He's probably going to spin a serve to my backhand and come in, so I'd better dip my return to his feet."

"I'll stay back on my serve, but I'll go in on the first short ball he gives me (I'll approach on his weaker backhand, naturally, unless he's out of position for a forehand)."

"She's trying to outsteady me. Well, I know I can be just as steady as she is."

"I knew his backhand was a weak shot, but he never seems to miss it. At least that's the way it seems today. So I decided to hit to his hard forehand, figuring he's more likely to miss there."

"He'll probably want to come to the net, so I'd better keep my shots deep."

Do you see one thing in common in all these answers? All the players were thinking of tactics, not of their own strokes. It was as if they trusted themselves, trusted their strokes, to carry out the tactics they planned. They stroked while they thought. Or, as I said in the first chapter, they played while they were thinking. But it's important to remember that they were skilled players who *had learned their strokes earlier in practice* designed for that purpose.

However, consider these answers I received when I asked these same players what they were thinking about as they were about to play *specific shots* in those points.

The player who intended to dip his return to the net-rushing server's feet had this to say: "I remembered how you've been working with me to shorten my swing for this shot, so that's what I had in mind. I told myself to make a short, snappy slice; you know, the three 'S's' we worked out in practice."

The player who rallied after having served while waiting for the first short ball said, "I planned to use the forehand slice you showed me to spin the ball and to curve it low to his backhand." I tried to pinpoint his thoughts by asking what he was thinking about as he prepared to slice. He said, "I was reminding myself to hit the back of the ball, not the bottom of it, to correct my fault of popping it up to him." When asked if that didn't give him a lot to think about, he said, "Not really; it was just 'hit the back, not the bottom.'"

The woman who decided to match her opponent in steadiness had to hit as many as eight, ten or twelve shots in many rallies to do so. When I asked what she was thinking about as she made those shots, she said, "Pretty much the same thing all the time: clear the barrier, get the ball up, easy up and over: all those things that work for me in our 'rally to your age' practice. (Author's note: We often had team members rallying to make as many consecutive shots as their age. When they reached that number, eighteen for an eighteen year old, let's say, they were permitted to increase their pace, to risk a little more, to attempt to force errors from the opponent).

One player whose shots were flat or were spinning only during baseline rallies told of a conscious adjustment he made to prepare for the top-spin passing shots he made against a net man. "I remembered to relax my wrist so I'd get my racket below the ball."

Other players said things like, "I thought about bringing my right shoulder through so I could guide my racket along the line." Another said, "I saw to it that I straightened my arm and that I bent my knees to get down to the ball," after he passed a net man with a top-spin backhand drive.

Do you see the different kinds of thinking going on here? These players thought first about the general tactical situation and about the tactics they figured would work best for them. But when it came to making a specific shot during those tactics, most of them quickly shifted their attention to some point of form. Not just any point of form, however, but one that they discovered earlier, in practice, worked for them. They thought about what they intended to do.

This is important and needs emphasis: They found out what works in practice. Then they used that same point of form in play whenever possible or necessary.

To motivate them in their practice I reminded them time and time again that they shouldn't expect to make a particular shot on a crucial point in play if they can't make it in our relaxed no-pressure practice sessions. With that explanation, it was easy enough to get them to work on their shots. Now let me explain how we practiced.

The first man learned to shorten his swing by standing with his back against a fence while I served softly to him from his own service line. The fence stopped his backswing and he quickly became aware of the muscle contractions necessary to stop his racket from crashing into it when he swung. After only a few minutes, during which time we emphasized that he was to make himself sensitive (muscle sense, again) to the physical changes required for that "new" swing, he stood in the regular receiver's location and was able to use his improved swing against a server.

That, however, was only the beginning. He practiced that swing almost daily for weeks, against teammates who were practicing their serves at the same time. After a few weeks, he was able to make that swing subconsciously even in critical play situations. As he explained, he told himself to make a short, snappy slice. From that point, his muscle sense took over to make the stroke he planned. A directive from his command center (his brain): compliance by his "troops" (his muscles) — that was the sequence.

The second player learned to hit the back of the ball by developing sensitivity in his wrist position. He learned to set it and the racket properly to place the racket on the back of the ball. For several successive days he practiced that shot with the new wrist position, while hitting against our practice board. Whenever he mistakenly set his wrist and racket wrongly, he hit the bottom of the ball causing it

When hitting a ball, only a single force is applied to it. But if your racket faces in one plane (let's say straight ahead, as Yannick Noah's does here), and moves in another plane (perhaps diagonally upward, as we see here), your swing has the same effect as two forces, one acting horizontally, the other vertically. The ball will go somewhere between the two (the direction will be the resultant of the two forces) but always more toward where your racket faces. Learn to consider the effect of such forces as you plan your stroke. You're likely to hit more accurately when you do. The swing thought for this kind of shot may be to simply "pull the racket up off the back of the ball."

to strike too high on the board. Once the ball sailed completely over the board. Needless to say, the visual impact of that error was impressive. In a week or so he was able to make that shot without thinking much about it even in actual play—except to recognize the tactical situation, the time to use it.

As for the woman groundstroker, the steady rallier, she learned to swing up and to hit up by changing the positions of her shoulders on both her forehand and backhand. She had been lowering her front shoulders during her backswings "to point them at the ball," as a teacher once told her to do. I can only assume the pointing was to ensure shoulder rotation but she mistakenly lowered the shoulder while rotating. As a result her racket was raised behind her, often too high to permit her to swing up to the ball. Simply by lowering her *rear* shoulder she had a lower backswing and a lower racket.

The change was almost instantaneous, though not permanent: a low to high swing resulting in lofted shots that almost always cleared the net. Daily practice with constant attention to lowering the rear shoulder eventually made this point of form a regular part of her swing.

With these examples, you can see how seriously our players practiced. They had their thinking caps on. They analyzed the game rationally, through conscious, deliberate thought. This led them to accept some fundamental facts of stroke production and to appreciate that there are sound reasons for stroking in a particular way. They learned to apply some principles of body mechanics and of aerodynamics in their stroke practice. And, through this combination of repetition with conscious thought, they were able to build strokes that were suitable for match play at their level. All of this we recognize as normal function of the brain. They were thinking players. Or perhaps it's more accurate to say they were thinking practicers.

With additional practice, they learned to make the stroke almost automatically, with only a minimum of conscious thought. They learned to shut off the thinking mechanisms and to let their muscle sense take over, which left their minds free to think about the tactics and strategies that would let them use their strokes to best advantage.

My intention in this book is to encourage you to practice and to learn to play as those players did. With a minimum of technical information that I'll provide in the next two chapters you will be able to understand what happens when you hit the ball. By applying the principles of mechanics I list there you'll be able to change your strokes, if only slightly, to make them more efficient. And with additional practice you, too, will learn to control your thought processes so that you can stroke at some appropriate low level of consciousness.

Now you may be thinking that all this is easier said than done. But you've probably already done it several times in life in other activities. Recall learning to skate or to ride a bike or to drive a car, or to play the piano or the guitar, or to shoot a basket. When first learning to do any of those things, you had to concentrate on a few technical things and could think of nothing else at the time. But gradually, with practice, you learned to make the physical moves almost automatically so that now you can think of other things while shooting or riding or playing. I'm suggesting you can learn to do the same in tennis.

The remaining chapters in this book are intended for that purpose. There I will describe how you can practice efficiently by using cues and imagery to prompt yourself to respond properly. I will also describe some gimmicks and gadgets that will help you develop the feel of good form. In addition, I'll suggest that you use your mind to fully understand what you are doing and why you are doing it. When you do put your mind to the learning tasks, you will be well on your way to becoming a thinking player, well on your way to better strokes and better shots, to more successful and more enjoyable play.

SUMMARY. Good form, good strokes, and good shots don't just occur naturally. Instead, the form that is likely to result in consistently good strokes is best developed in practice, where you think about various points, or features, of that form. In practice, think about what you are doing as you stroke. In play, however, think ahead about what you intend to do. Then trust your body to do it.

CHAPTER 3

BUILD YOUR STROKES SCIENTIFICALLY

ooooooooooooooooooooooooooooooooooo

You are more likely to become a thinking player if you understand and apply some simple facts of body mechanics in your play. It will help if you understand (1) what happens when your racket meets the ball, (2) what happens to the ball after it leaves your racket, and (3) what you are capable of doing physically as you swing.

For this kind of information we turn to a relatively new area of study in athletics—biomechanics. From it you can get a background of facts and figures that will help you understand your swing and will help you determine how best to shape it into an effective stroke.

The science of biomechanics explains and describes the effects of muscular forces you use to swing your racket. And it explains how to hold your racket to produce the particular shot you have in mind.

IMPACT GEOMETRY

When planning a shot, pay attention to what is likely to happen at impact. The direction of the ball's rebound off your racket is determined by the combined effects of several factors: the setting of your racket face (is it facing left or right, up or down?); the direction in which your racket is moving (are you swinging parallel to the ground or diagonally upward or downward?); the spin on the ball; and the angle at which the ball is approaching.

Let's first consider the matter of controlling the left-to-right direction of your shot. When you intend to hit directly back to where the ball came from, make your racket face in that direction, perpendicular to the ball's line of approach. Since the ball approaches your racket perpendicularly, it will rebound perpendicularly, toward where the racket faces.

When you swing softly and your intention is to angle the ball away from the line of its approach, you'll have to allow for the ball's tendency to deflect off your racket at almost the same angle it came to it. If you don't want to angle your shot that sharply you must make your racket face somewhere between the line of the ball's approach and the line of departure you want.

When you hit hard and make the force of your swing dominant over the force of the oncoming ball, the ball will flatten against your strings more than it does when you hit softly. As a result, it will deflect off your racket at an angle closer to 90 degrees than to the normal angle of deflection. You can then make your racket face more directly toward your target. And the harder you hit, the more this is so.

Now let's consider how to control the up-and-down flight of the ball. If a ball approaches your racket horizontally, i.e., not rising or falling, and if your racket face is perpendicular to it and is moving directly into it, the ball will leave your racket along a line

For maximum efficiency and control, flatten the arc of your forward swing as shown here. Start your swing with your arm bent, then straighten it as you go into your follow through.

perpendicular to your racket and parallel to the ground. This is an effective way to swing at a high-bouncing ball that you can meet at the peak of its bounce above the height of the net.

If the ball is rising as you hit, it will tend to deflect upward off your racket face unless you close your racket slightly and/or swing slightly downward to it. If the ball is dropping as you hit, it will deflect downward off your racket unless you open the face and swing in an upward plane. In these cases the degree to which you adjust the setting of your racket face and/or the plane of your swing should depend on the angle at which the ball approaches your racket and the angle of flight you want off your racket. The greater the angle of approach from horizontal, the bigger adjustments you must make. Be aware, however, that if you change only your swing plane, the ball will start off higher than where your racket faces but the topspin imparted to it by the upward swing may cause it to curve downward and therefore land shorter than you intended.

For a topspin shot your racket must be moving upward from an imaginary plane perpendicular to the strings. The upward swing will make the ball go higher than where your racket faces but lower than the plane in which it is moving. For a backspin shot your racket must be moving downward from a plane perpendicular to the strings. As a result, the ball will go lower than where your racket faces but higher than the plane in which it is moving.

With all these variables operating at impact, the flight of the ball is not easy to control or predict. We may generalize, however, and say that the ball's flight will be the result of the components of force acting on it. The more successfully you control some force components and the more accurately you allow for others, the more accurately you are likely to hit. But to finish this discussion of impact geometry on a practical note, let me say that the harder you swing at the ball, the less allowance you need make for the angle of incidence and the angle of reflection.

GRIPS

To hit consistently accurate groundstrokes you have to set your racket properly. To a large extent, your racket's setting is a function of your grips.

Regardless of how you hold your racket, check your grips to see if they meet the following criteria. First, they should be comfortable. Second, they should allow you to move your racket quickly into your stroke pattern. Third, they should enable you to hold your racket firmly enough to resist the force of the oncoming ball.

There is also a fourth requirement that is just as important and yet is often overlooked. I'm referring to sensitivity. Your grips should provide sufficient sensitivity, sufficient "feel" for you to know where your racket is facing at impact. Why? Recall my earlier discussion of impact geometry: The direction of the ball's flight off your racket is determined jointly by the direction in which your strings are facing and the direction in which your racket is moving—and nearer the former if they differ. This applies to both left-to-right and up-and-down flight. Obviously, the setting of your racket is one of the most important variables you must contend with as you stroke.

If you are having trouble controlling the trajectories of your shots, you are probably not setting that face properly. This may be because your grip does not provide enough sensitivity. You may be better off changing your grip slightly to one that enables you to sense the position of your racket more accurately so you can set it more accurately. Experiment to find that grip.

First, give yourself a simple test. Using your present grip, extend your arm and racket at waist height. Then, rotate your arm and racket continually in alternate directions—first, clockwise, then counter-clockwise. While still rotating, close your eyes. Stop rotating and quickly try to set your racket face into an edge-down position, perpendicular to the ground. Open your eyes to check for accuracy.

Next, change your grip slightly by moving your hand clockwise and/or counter-clockwise from where you normally place it on the handle. With each new change adjust your hand carefully to make it feel comfortable. Now, with your hand in each new, different position, give yourself the eyes-closed test to see which grip lets you set the racket face accurately.

Then while on the court find the best grip. With a practice partner, rally across the net. Again, experiment with all the grips that worked well for you in the eyes-closed test. Aim your shots at various heights and at various places in your partner's court. Pay special attention to how well you can control the height of your shots with each of the different grips. After a reasonable amount of time you should be able to decide which grip lets you hit most accurately.

As an example of personal preferences in grips, I point out that Smith, Nastase, Borg, and Evert all hold their rackets differently. Yet all hold them correctly because each one of them has found the grip that works best for him or her. Practice to find your own best grip.

Marty Davis, a collegiate All-American player, has learned to set his racket face vertically (as if it is "standing on edge") as it passes through the hitting area. This can be managed with a variety of grips. Players are urged to find their own "best" grip, the one that provides adequate sensitivity for setting the racket properly.

WRIST ACTION

Left-to-right control of your shots depends on proper racket settings, too. Even while allowing for the other variables that operate at impact, you must finally set your racket so that its facing will provide the rebound angle you need to hit toward your aim point.

You will probably hit more accurately if you eliminate wrist action as you swing. Instead of moving your hand at the wrist, set your wrist firmly in what is called the "laid-back" position, one that keeps your strings facing your target as your racket passes through your hitting area. High-speed photos reveal that a laid-back wrist is one of the most common points of form among players known to have good groundstrokes. It permits them to have a contact area in which to meet the ball rather than only one contact point. And it accounts in large measure for the high degree of accuracy of the strokes. If you are not familiar with the laid-back wrist, you can learn it easily with the following gimmick.

Stand in a hitting position alongside the net (as if to hit across the net) and press your racket face against it. Bend your wrist back to keep your racket handle and your racket face parallel to the net. Then, while keeping your wrist in that laid-back position, draw your racket back away from the net and then quickly swing it forward to the net, hitting the net band squarely with your racket face. Repeat the swing several times, trying to whack the net band with your racket face as if you were beating a rug.

During actual play and practice, make your wrist look and feel as it does during this exercise. At the critical moment, when your racket meets the ball, keep your wrist in the laid-back position to make your strings face your intended target.

You will notice that I have not been specific about the degree to which you should lay your wrist back, except to say that your strings should face your target. Practice adjusting your wrist for the different shots you intend to make in the varying play situations that occur in a match. Try to tailor each swing to the situation, laying your wrist back more or less depending on your intended direction. But don't let your wrist flip loosely. You can prevent that simply by holding your racket firmly. A firm wrist at impact is another common fundamental in the game.

You can prove to yourself how this works. Extend your hitting arm and your racket opposite your belt buckle as if you are hitting a waist-high forehand. Then, with loose wrist action, quickly move your hand back and forth in a kind of fish-tail motion. Next, squeeze your racket tightly and try to repeat the fish-tail motion. You will find it hard to do because movement at the wrist is restricted when the grip is made firm. The tendons of the flexor muscles of the fingers—those

Martina Navratilova is shown hitting a low backhand volley. With the soft stroke used for this shot, the ball's angle of approach to her racket (diagonally downward) will cause the ball to deflect slightly downward from her racket unless she adjusts her racket's setting to prevent that. Here she has beveled her racket (opened it) to gain enough lift for her shot to clear the net. Though she should not be thinking of this while doing it, certainly she should plan to do it as she recognizes the need for it. So should you when you need to make similar shots. (Photo by Cheryl Traendly)

used to make a fist—are worked from the forearm and pass over the wrist in a way that restricts motion there. So for a firm wrist, hold a firm grip.

But wrist movement is often related to grip strength. If you have strong hands, you can grip relatively less tightly than another player with weak hands and still have adequate control of your racket. And, as you squeeze less tightly, you will be able to have freer wrist movement. In other words, there is not one specific amount of wrist action that works efficiently for everyone. Instead, we see players hit effectively with varying amounts of motion at the wrist, which means, of course, that you can experiment to find your own best combination of grip pressure and wrist mobility.

Besides permitting hand action in a left-to-right direction, your wrist also allows up-and-down motion. And so you should consider which positions provide maximum efficiency, especially for swings made at low balls.

Analysis of good groundstrokers swinging at low balls reveals that their wrists are seldom cocked. But neither are they relaxed so much as to permit their rackets to dangle loosely from their hands. This last position, let's call it a rounded wrist, does not permit a firm grip, and usually results in poor racket control and inaccurate hitting. Stop-action photos of good strokers show that their wrists are usually fixed in a position somewhere between those two extremes.

You can find your own best wrist position by experimenting in the following manner. Hold your racket with your backhand grip and extend your arm and racket opposite your mid-section as if to hit a waist-high groundstroke. Now with your other hand, press down on the back of your hitting hand. Press hard enough to form the rounded wrist I described earlier, the one that does not permit you to hold your racket firmly. Then gradually reduce the pressure on your hitting hand and raise the racket slowly with wrist action. Try to make a tight grip at various stages as your racket comes up. You will be able to feel how much you must straighten your wrist from the rounded position in order to hold your racket firmly. In actual play, you need to raise your wrist only that amount. Your wrist may or may not be cocked. Your racket face may or may not be higher than your wrist. Neither of these matters. What does matter is that you set your wrist in a position that permits you to hold your racket firmly.

ARM ACTION

Motion in your swing is the result of the muscular force you apply to your body's system of levers. In biomechanics, the term "lever" refers to a long bone or a combination of bones, fixed at one end and free to move at the other. When you move your upper arm at the shoulder, or your lower arm at the elbow, or your hand at the wrist, you see levers in motion. They function in a way that enables you to generate considerable momentum at their movable ends while moving only a slight amount at their fixed ends. When you hold your racket in your hand, it becomes part of this chain of levers and so you can impart momentum to the ball.

You can use one particular characteristic of levers in motion to determine how best to swing your arm during a stroke. If you keep your arm locked straight during a swing, your racket will be travelling in an arc. And, in the arc it will be facing your target only momentarily. And worse yet, it will be moving toward your target only momentarily. You will probably hit more accurately if you learn to flatten the arc of your swing.

You can do this by starting your swing with a bent arm and by making it straighter as your racket moves into the ball. From the point of view of mechanics, you will then be making a two-lever swing, with your upper arm moving at the shoulder and your lower arm moving at the elbow. With that kind of swing you can change the customary circular path that results from a one-lever swing to a straight-line path that is characteristic of most two-lever motions. With your racket moving properly toward your target area, you will almost certainly hit more accurately. And this applies to both forehands and backhands.

True, a two-lever swing creates an additional moving part and so may be more complicated. But it offers a second advantage, particularly on the backhand, that often offsets that disadvantage.

When you bend your arm at the elbow during your backswing, you can then use motion at that joint as a source of power, just as a martial arts expert does on a karate chop. When you swing your arm at the shoulder and also straighten it at the elbow, that combination of moves may enable you to generate more force than you can with a straight-armed, one-lever swing.

Whether hitting a forehand or a backhand, you can make other adjustments to help flatten the arc of your swing. Whenever possible, turn your hips and shoulders toward the net and step toward the net with your front foot. These points of form are universally accepted among experienced teachers and are usually described as "pivoting" and "stepping into the shot."

In fast play, however, you will not always be able to swing with such ideal form. When you can't step in and can't pivot, the burden of flattening the arc of your swing falls on your arm. And so you must make an adjustment. As your racket comes into the ball, make a conscious attempt to move your hitting arm away from your body rather than in an arc. Remember, the racket's movement and its setting determine where the ball goes. For accurate hitting, swing toward your target, not toward a sideline. Flatten the arc of your swing.

You face this problem when hitting from an open stance as well, with your body facing the net. In that posture you will have a tendency to pull your racket across the ball. If you don't want that effect, make the adjustment. When you learn to do it regularly, you will begin to feel comfortable in an open stance, especially on your forehand. You may begin to prefer an open stance on that shot (as many players do) except on those few occasions when you want to hit with maximum force.

BACKSWING

Though I may appear to be misplacing this discussion of backswings by having it come after the descripion of the forward swing, I do so for good reason. In my method of flexible instruction I stress how to hit the ball more than merely how to swing at it. Or, to say it differently, I stress what happens at impact and I suggest that a learner's mind should be centered on what happens there, at the "moment of truth," so to speak. Variations of the backswing are permissible and even encouraged as I will show here. But there can be no deviations from the proper way to *hit* the ball, ie., to place the racket on it. Hence my discussion of the forward swing comes first.

Just as I suggested you do with your grips, experiment with different kinds of backswings on your groundstrokes. If you don't already use it, try a straight, flat swing. It's the simplest kind to make and for that reason may be the best one for you. But try to combine your backswing and your forward swing into one continuous motion. Adjust the speed of your backswing in accord with the amount of time you have to make it. Don't get your racket back so that you have to pause while waiting for the ball. Such a jerky, start-stop-and-start again swing is less efficient than the smoother, fluent, continuous swing used by most good groundstrokers.

However, you may be more comfortable making a circular backswing, a loop. From your ready posture, carry the racket upward and backward to start your backswing. Move your racket in an egg-shaped pattern, up and back, down and around, then forward into the ball.

During your forehand backswing, you may keep your elbow down or you may raise it. Either method works, and both are used by ranking players. By keeping your elbow down, you can simplify your swing. This may be reason enough for keeping your elbow in this position; it may enable you to set the racket face properly at contact—flat, vertical, standing on edge. If you raise your elbow, the hitting surface of your racket will slant downward, and you will have to make adjustments in your elbow and wrist positions to bring the face into the ball properly. This is not the easiest and most efficient way to hit, but it will enable you to generate a great deal of racket speed. If you can manage to control this kind of swing, it may be the best kind for you.

On the backhand groundstroke we see far more straight backswing than circular ones for the reason that it appears to be more natural. As you turn to start your backswing, your racket will start to move back, too. Carry-through with that action, extending your arm slightly to move your racket tip back toward the rear fence. Simultaneously bring your hitting hand in close to your rear hip and you'll be in good position to start your forward swing.

But, as I suggested on the forehand, you may prefer making a slight loop here, too, and for the same reason: to gain the advantage of continuous motion. Either may work for you and each is worth experimenting with.

Whichever method you use, start your backswing as soon as you determine the direction of the ball as it comes off your opponent's racket. If you merely have to turn to reach the ball, make the backswing as you turn. If you have to run to reach a wide ball, start your backswing later. Use your arms in a natural running motion, but start your backswing as you get close to the ball.

THE TWO-HANDED BACKHAND

If you feel uncomfortable on your backhands, particularly with your grip, and if you are unhappy with your stroke, experiment with a two-handed swing. You may find that you have sufficient dexterity in your left hand to be able to use it to your advantage in support of your right hand. You'll then not have to change from your comfortable forehand grip though it may not be suitable for backhands. The supporting left hand can compensate for the "weak" position of your right one.

When swinging with two hands you have several options as regards grips. If we consider that you can place either hand in any of three locations on the handle—Western, Eastern, and Continental—you see that you have nine possible combinations. Which then should you use? The logical approach is to experiment to see which combination of grips helps you best meet the criteria I mentioned earlier. But here I suggest again, be specially attentive to sensitivity so you'll choose grips that let you set your racket face properly for your shots.

As you experiment, start with the grip combination that seems to work best for the majority of two-handers. While maintaining your normal forehand grip place your left palm flat against the back plane of the handle and above the right hand, i.e., closer to the strings. As you close your left hand on the handle you'll be setting it in the Eastern grip. This grip will probably provide most sensitivity because you can relate the feel of your palm to the postion of your hitting surface. As your palm faces, so will your strings face.

The two-handed grip lets you use a kind of double wrist action to generate racket speed. You can pull with your right hand while also pushing with the left.

But you can use your wrists differently in a kind of "couple" arrangement to get racket speed, too. As you start your forward swing, push against the handle with your right hand while simultaneously pushing the handle with your left. These two forces working against each other will move the racket in a circular path around your hands with more speed than you could generate single-handedly.

You may also use the couple action to get additional top-spin on your shots. As your racket approaches the ball, push down on the handle with your right hand while also pushing up with the left. You'll again get more racket speed than you could with one hand alone; this time in a diagonally upward plane. The result will be a top-spin drive.

If maximum accuracy, rather than speed, is your objective on a particular shot, eliminate as much wrist action as you can. Recall my description of the laid-back wrist on the forehand. Here then, consider that your two-handed backhand is like a one-handed left-handed forehand. For this you would maintain the laid-back position in your LEFT wrist. Use it on your two-handed, too, for the same reason: It's the accurate way to hit. With this kind of swing, let the right hand merely go along for the ride, so to speak, letting it merely assist in support of the left hand.

On the two-handed backhands you may use the normal sources of power—arm and elbow action, body rotation, and weight transfer. But here you must time your body rotation differently from what I describe for a one-handed backhand. Since your intention is to bring your left arm and hand through the contact area, you must turn your body out of the way just as you do for regular forehands. It's a simple matter of mechanics that is seen in high-speed photos of all good two-handed shots. Make your collar buttons face the net before contact so you can flatten the arc of your swing as you must for consistently accurate hitting. (see page 144).

You'll find that you can't turn your body soon enough if your rear foot (the left one) remains firmly on the ground. Instead, you'll have to turn and twist that foot clockwise to let only the outside edge of it remain on the ground. Or, you may lift it off the ground completely. Either of these adjustments will let you have the unrestricted body action you need for both accuracy and speed. With those descriptions of the foot adjustments, you may recall seeing Jimmy Connors in the first posture (rear foot turned to its outside edge) and Chris Evert in the second (rear foot off the ground). Their two-handed shots are perfect examples of how these foot adjustments are to be made in play. Try both to see which works best for you.

THE SERVICE TOSS

You have your choice between a one-lever motion and a two-lever one when tossing the ball to serve, too. And again, each method has its advantages.

With a one-lever motion you'll be using fewer moving parts. That's why most top-level players toss that way. They extend their tossing arms fully and they keep them that way throughout the toss.

But here again, a one-lever motion will move your hand and the ball in an arc. The direction of your toss will then be affected by the movement of your hand. If you release the ball early, below waist height, you'll toss too far forward because your tossing hand will be moving forward in that part of the arc. If you release the ball late, at head height, for example, you'll toss it back too far because your tossing hand will be moving back. For an accurate toss you'll have to release the ball at only that one point in the arc at which your tossing hand is moving straight up.

To minimize the circular path that results naturally from the one-lever tossing motion, you can make two adjustments. Shift your weight on to your front foot during your toss. And move your front shoulder up as your tossing hand moves up.

But you may still have trouble finding the right release point and timing the weight shift properly. If so, you may toss more accurately by using a two-lever motion. For this, start your toss with your arm bent at the elbow. Then while swinging your entire arm at the shoulder socket, straighten it at the elbow. You can then move your tossing hand in a straight line, straight up, rather than in the arc described earlier. And with your hand moving in the proper direction throughout your tossing motion, you may release the ball at any point in that motion and still toss accurately. You see that this effect is similar to what you do when you hit groundstrokes with a bent arm that is straightening as you go into your followthrough. You flatten the arc. Here the arc of your tossing hand is in a vertical plane.

But I remind you that wrist action has the same effect on your tossing hand as it does on your hitting hand during groundstrokes. Your hand will be facing different directions during the action. And since the ball will go wherever your hand is facing, it is not likely to go to the right spot very often.

You already know how to correct this problem. Set your tossing wrist in the laid-back position I described for groundstrokes. Bend your wrist back to make the back of your palm parallel to the ground. Your palm will then be facing directly upward. And so when you release the ball, it will go in that same direction, straight up to the spot you intended.

All of my suggestions in this chapter are intended to help you develop control and accuracy. To summarize, we can say that the keys to accuracy are a laid-back wrist combined with movement along a line toward the target, both when hitting and when tossing.

AERODYNAMICS

The direction of the ball's flight off your racket is determined almost instantly. Several studies have shown the contact to last for only milliseconds (.0038—.005 seconds). It takes much longer than that for you to feel the hit. And it takes even more time for your brain to order your hands to modify the stroke if you want to. You see, then, how critical the setting of your racket is. That's why I stress that you be attentive to its setting during practice so you learn to make that adjustment with just an instant's thought during play. You will then be free to attend to other points of tactics and strategy.

But you must be equally attentive to the plane of your swing. Should you swing level (parallel to the ground)? Upward or downward? It all depends on your intention. A level swing will result in a flat shot, one with little or no spin, if your racket faces the same direction your racket is moving. A swing in an upward or downward plane will result in a spin shot if your racket isn't facing the same direction as those planes.

Topspin

When you hit the ball an upward, glancing blow, with the plane of your swing upward from the plane in which your racket faces, you will put topspin on the ball. Topspin makes the ball curve downward and drop sooner than it would from the force of gravity alone. You can use it to advantage against a net player when you want to keep the ball low. You can also use it for full-length drives when you want to hit very hard with some degree of safety. The spin will help keep the ball in the court.

Principles of physics, of mechanics, operate here, too. When you hit a ball, gravity begins to act on it immediately. You may control your shots better if you understand the effects of gravity. If you hit a ball horizontally, parallel to the ground, after it leaves your racket it will descend one foot in one-fourth second and four feet in one-half second from the effects of gravity alone ($D = 1/2gt^2$, where g = gravity and t = time). Obviously, when hitting a high ball you must hit it hard enough to reach the net before gravity pulls it down into the court. And you must loft low balls to make them clear the net despite the effects of gravity and top-spin. On these lofted shots, top-spin can help bring the ball down *after* it has cleared the net.

On a topspin shot, the top surface of the ball rotates forward and

(A)

(B)

APPLYING TOPSPIN: The author shown demonstrating a "gimmick" useful to teach the concept of topspin. He presses a ball against the net band with his racket. After holding it there momentarily, he pulls his racket up quickly to drag the ball up and off the net. As a result of his pulling motion the ball will have topspin. The student then imitates his motions and later applies the feeling of the upward pull in his strokes.

downward, while the bottom surface rotates backward. The bottom surface drags much of the air near the front of the ball around with it, and the effect is to speed up the flow of air relative to the speed of flow over the top of the ball. The faster flowing air at the bottom exerts less pressure against the ball than does the slower moving air at the top. The net result of this difference in pressure is the downward curve characteristic of topspinning balls. This explanation is in accord with the principle formulated by Daniel Bernoulli, the 18th century Swiss scientist, which states that pressure in a fluid decreases with increased velocity of the fluid. The ball's curving from the effect of spin is known as the "Magnus effect," after the German scientist who is credited with first noting it and describing it.

Topspin makes the ball bounce lower, faster, and farther, except when the spin makes the ball curve very sharply downward. In that case, the bounce may be higher than if the ball were not spinning. Topspin makes the ball deflect upward off a volleyer's racket unless the spin makes the oncoming ball arch sharply downward. In that case, the arc may neutralize the effect of spin.

You can use the effects of spin to your advantage when serving, too. Here, try to apply a combination of top-spin and side-spin. For this, hit the ball an upward glancing blow while your racket is moving across the ball in a left-to-right direction. The upward direction will give you top-spin, of course: the left-to-right direction, side-spin. For reasons I've already explained, the top-spin will give the ball an exaggerated downward curve (hopefully, after the ball has first cleared the net), so that the ball will approach the ground in a more nearly vertical angle than would a non-spinning ball. The side-spin will curve the ball to the receiver's right but will cause it to bounce toward his or her left, toward the backhand. The result of this combination of spins, the high bounce to the backhand, is usually the most effective placement of the serve.

When hitting with top-spin to cause a high bounce, you must actually make the ball travel up off your racket, not down as is generally supposed about the serve. Obviously, if you intend to hit up, you can't meet the ball at the full extension of your reach. Instead, you must meet it at a slightly lower point, and it is while you are extending to full stretch that you should make contact with the ball. You may do this by hitting either before your arm is fully extended or before your wrist action brings your racket into alignment with your forearm.

With practice you can learn to vary the degree to which you swing up and across the ball. You can also learn to adjust your wrist to place your racket properly on the ball. By adjusting these variables along with the force of your swing, you can vary the amount of spin you put on the ball.

Backspin

You apply backspin when you hit the ball a glancing blow while the plane of your swing is downward from the plane your racket faces. Backspin acts in precisely the opposite manner of topspin and causes the ball to stay in flight longer. The lift provided by backspin neutralizes the pull of gravity somewhat and makes the ball appear to "sail" or "float" until it loses momentum. Here, the top surface of the ball moves backward, dragging some of the nearby air around with it. The faster moving air exerts less pressure than does the slower moving air at the bottom surface of the ball. The greater air pressure against the bottom surface causes the lift that is characteristic of cuts, chops, and slices.

You may use the additional lift provided by the spin to give your opponents difficult balls to handle. If as you hit the ball a downward glancing blow (to impart backspin), you make contact directly behind the ball (rather than toward the bottom of it) you can send the ball off your racket in a flat trajectory. It will then approach the ground at a shallow angle. And since the angle of incidence (almost) equals the angle of deflection, the ball will leave the ground at a shallow angle. In other words, it will take a low, skidding bounce that many players find difficult to handle, especially on the backhand. For this reason, you may effectively use the slice as an approach shot, following it to the net to intercept your opponent's returns.

You may also vary the amount of backspin to disturb your opponent's stroke rhythm. By swinging more or less downward you can change the amount of backspin you put on the ball. And by meeting the ball more or less toward its bottom you can change the trajectory of your shot. When you change one or both of these variables on successive strokes, and when you mix these kinds of shots with flat ones and with topspin shots, you'll be forcing your opponent to adjust to varying speeds, trajectories and bounces. Many of your opponents will find this unsettling. Strokes that they practiced so hard to groove seem no longer to work for them.

If you apply backspin and hit quite a lot under the ball—and also hit softly—you can make the ball drop nearly vertically and close to the net. The combined effects of the angle of incidence and the backspin will cause the ball to bounce vertically or nearly so. The result may often be a point-winning drop-shot, one that your opponent can't reach before its second bounce!

Backspin makes the ball deflect downward off a volleyer's racket. But you can reduce the effect of your opponent's backspin (and often negate it completely) by volleying crisply with a firm grip. The force of your swing may then be dominant over the force of the spinning ball. Now, though the direction of the rebound will be the resultant of the two forces, with unequal forces it will be closer to the direction of the dominant force: in this case, the direction your racket faces.

We can summarize this discussion of spin by saying the amount of spin you impart to the ball is determined partly by the size of the angle between the plane of your swing and the slant of your racket face. The force of your swing also affects it. These you can vary as your intention to apply more or less spin varies.

This discussion of the mechanics of strokes is intended to increase your technical knowledge. With that as a background you should be able to understand the reason for your misses and for your good shots. And so you can deduce what corrections to make on succeeding shots to reduce the number of your misses. These are the first steps to becoming a thinking player: knowing what to do differently and knowing how to do it. Or, to put it in different words, making conscious corrections rather than waiting for them to occur automatically.

I continue this discussion of stroke mechanics in the following chapter. There, however, I'll suggest ways you can use mechanical principles to develop power in your swings and speed in your shots.

SUMMARY. Technical knowledge of stroke can help you develop good strokes. Technical knowledge can help you understand the reason for your misses and for your good shots. As you learn to stroke in accordance with selected principles of movement you almost certainly will begin to stroke more accurately.

CHAPTER 4

ADD SPEED SCIENTIFICALLY

○○○○○○○○○○○○○○○○○○○○○○○○○○○○○○○○○○○

In the preceding chapter I made suggestions for using the body's lever system as you practice to build your strokes. My emphasis there was on accuracy. I continue that discussion here noting additional mechanical principles that may help you hit harder.

REDUCE RACKET RESISTANCE

As you complete your backswing and start your forward swing, your racket tends to travel in a circular path. As it moves in that path it offers a certain amount of resistance, and you have to apply muscular force to overcome its resistance.

In circular motion, the amount of resistance offered by the racket depends not only on its weight but also on its distance from the center of the turn, from a point in your upper body around which you move your arm, hand, and racket. The closer the racket is to the center of the turn, the less resistance it offers. In technical terms, one can say its rotational inertia (or moment of inertia, if you prefer) is reduced.

You can apply this principle to your advantage by keeping your arm bent as you start your forward swing. Your racket then will be easier to swing. You'll need less force to move it, and as a result, you'll have more force available for speed.

We often see this principle applied in other sports. In figure skating, the skater pulls her arms and her free leg in close to her body to gain speed as she spins. To slow down, she extends her arms and legs. And in aquatics, a diver tucks for the same reason: to gain speed for spins and flips. If the body is spinning too fast for the kind of entry planned, the diver "opens up" to slow the spinning motion.

You apply this principle, perhaps unknowingly, when you "scratch your back" while serving. You bend your arm while making your preparatory swing to reduce the racket's resistance to turning. You can then swing it faster and with less effort than you can with a straight arm.

You can apply this principle when returning serves, too. To prove how it works, do this experiment. Stand at the net, about two feet from it and with your back toward it as if you are to return a serve hit toward you from that baseline. First extend your arms fully and then swing your racket back as fast as you can to hit the net band behind you. After several swings, change your ready posture slightly. Bend your arms at the elbows and hold your elbows close against your sides. Then make several backswings, again hitting the net band as fast as you can. Almost certainly you'll see that you hit the net more quickly with the bent arm (short radius) swing.

The lesson of this experiment is plain. When receiving serves, hold your elbows close against your sides to shorten the length of the arm-racket lever. You'll then need less force to move it and so more force will be available for speed, here for speed of both the forward swing and the back swing.

SWING A LONG LEVER

You can combine a second mechanical principle with the first to gain even more racket speed as you serve. If we again consider the body as a lever system, we can say that for a constant angular speed, the speed of the turning motion at the end of the lever is proportional to the length of the lever.

The analogy of a turning wheel helps explain this principle. Imagine several points located on a spoke of the wheel, each point a different distance from the axle. Now you can see that the points farther out from the axle move through the same angle and in the same period of time as do the closer-in points. But, obviously they are moving a greater linear distance. We have to conclude, therefore, that they are moving faster. And, the farther out a point is, the faster it moves. Actually, its speed is proportional to its distance (in this case, its radius) from the axle, the center of the turn.

To understand how this applies in tennis, use this bit of imagery. Imagine you are swinging a 12-inch ruler through an arc of 90 degrees at a certain speed. Next pretend you are swinging a 36-inch ruler through the same distance (90 degrees) at the same speed. Here, both rulers are too light to offer any appreciable resistance to your turning motion. As a result, the end of the three-foot ruler would be moving three times as fast as the end of the one-foot ruler because it is three times farther from the center of the turn.

Now when serving, the weight of your racket and the weight of your arm offer resistance to your turning motion. But as I've described earlier, if you shorten the radius of that "lever" (by bending your arm to scratch your back) your arm and racket will offer less resistance. Then once you've attained adequate speed, if you can maintain that speed, straighten your arm to gain the advantage of the longer lever.

APPLY THE TIME-FORCE PRINCIPLE

As you practice to develop speed on your serves, consider that racket speed depends not only on the amount of force you apply but also on the time for which you apply force. A small force applied for a longer period of time can result in racket speed equal to that gained by a larger force applied for only a brief period.

This time-force principle suggests that you may serve with more force when you use a long, full backswing rather than a short, compact one. Let your racket flow down past your knees and up toward the top of the rear fence. When your arm is extended at shoulder

PRONATION DURING THE SERVE: With the racket shown immediately after contact on this serve, the hitter's arm can be seen in the pronated position. This action, when accompanied by upper arm rotation (medial rotation of the humerus) and by wrist action (extension followed by flexion) contributes to racket speed.

height behind you, bend it to bring your racket forward and down into the back-scratching position. If you bend your arm sooner during your backswing, you'll have less time to apply force. You'll probably serve at less than maximum speed as a result.

From the backscratch position, pull your racket up toward the ball. In this action, exert yourself; apply force vigorously to move the racket as fast as you can. As your racket gets close to the ball, straighten your arm and turn your forearm to make your palm and your racket face the net. This action, called pronating, adds speed to your racket and so adds speed to your serve.

You may understand pronating better by practicing this way. Stand sideways against a fence, as if you're going to serve into it, with your

An example of the kinetic chain being properly applied on a forehand. Note that the player has already shifted her weight to the front foot and has turned her hips out of the way, to the left. The shoulders will turn next and the racket will be dragged along by the arm as it moves with the shoulders. As these forces are added successively, momentum will be transferred outward from the axis of the turn to the arm and the racket. As a result the hitter will be able to make a forceful shot.

front foot pressed against the bottom of it. Move your racket up behind you as you do in a regular serving motion. As your racket comes close to the fence, quickly turn your forearm and wrist in a counterclockwise direction so you can hit the fence squarely with your entire racket face. Make several imaginary serves like that, gradually increasing the speed of your swings. Then stand at the baseline and serve across the net. Use that same pronating motion that let you hit the fence squarely. Now it will enable you to hit the ball squarely on its back side, on the nose of an imaginary face.

You can apply the time-force principle on groundstrokes too. A long, full backswing, whether circular or flat, will give you more time to generate force. But here you'll be wise to adjust your swings to make them consistent with your objectives on various shots. If you intend to hit hard, make a long swing, perhaps even a circular one to let the force of gravity contribute to racket speed. If you intend to hit softly, use a short, compact swing. And if you find a circular backswing difficult to control, use a straight one. With its stop-and-start motion you may be able to control your racket better and so hit more accurately, though with less force.

ADJUST THE FORCE OF YOUR SWINGS

Even as you adjust the length of your swings to alter the time during which you can apply force, you can also adjust the amount of force you apply at several joints.

On the forehand you can generate racket speed by (1) swinging your arm from the shoulder, (2) transferring your weight from your rear foot to your front foot, (3) turning your hips and shoulders, and (4) using wrist action. On the backhand you can add motion at the elbow to these sources. On both the forehand and backhand you can add knee action: Straighten your knees if you intend to hit an upward glancing blow (for topspin).

Use these forces in varying amounts depending on the purpose of each shot. You may not need all of them on a particular stroke. You may be able to eliminate body rotation and the shift of weight, and get sufficient force with arm and elbow action only.

But when you do want a great deal of speed in your shot, try a bit of sophisticated body action not often recognized. I'm referring to what can be called "reverse body action." On the forehand, it works like this.

Though you turn your shoulders clockwise and move your arm and racket with them into your backswing, they shouldn't move together as you start your forward swing. Step with your left foot (to shift your weight) and reverse your shoulder action (turn them counterclockwise) *while* your arm and racket continue to move back for the last foot or so of your backswing. Then whip the racket through the remainder of your backswing and into your forward swing. With such action, in which your body turns first and the arm and racket follow afterward, you'll be applying the forces successively, one after another, and not simultaneously. The result will be a whip-like swing and probably a faster shot.

You can use similar arm-and-body timing for power on your serve. As your racket reaches its high-point behind you, start your body rotation, i.e., the counterclockwise turn. Then bring your racket forward and downward behind you, whipping it through the backscratch position. From there, move it up into the ball by rotating your upper arm, by pronating your lower arm, by forcefully extending your arm at the elbow, and by flexing your wrist.

When serving you can use your body, your feet, and your legs to generate even more force upward. Raise your front shoulder during your toss, then reverse the shoulder positions as you turn your body to start your swing. Bend your knees as you pull your racket toward your back, then straighten them as you lower your racket into the backscratch position. Along with that knee action, extend your feet at the ankles.

When you apply maximum force at each of these joints, and when you apply these motions in the proper sequence and with proper timing, the combined forces may cause you to leave the ground as you hit. If so, so much the better.

Surely you've noticed that most good servers jump as they serve. While watching a world-class tournament recently I noticed that two out of three of them jump in one way or another. Some jump across the line to land on the rear foot, which was flung across the line during the swing. Their body action was part pivot and part jump. And the combination of forceful upward thrust and vigorous body rotation created a kind of rising spiral effect much like a figure skater executing a leaping spin.

Other jumpers used less body rotation and so landed on the front foot. Their emphasis was on upward thrust, and as a result that motion appeared to contribute a larger share to the total force generated than did body rotation.

If you are not now a jumper, try it. Try to apply so much force upward with your feet, legs, body, arm, and hand that your feet leave the ground instantly after impact.

My suggestion that you may add force to your serve by jumping may appear to be a denial of Newton's well known law of reaction. But the fact remains that a large majority of good servers do jump. There may be no logical explanation for this except to say that the racket is swung upward to meet the ball and so any motion that contributes to that upward thrust may help increase racket speed.

We see similar conflicts in other sports. High-speed photography reveals that most world-class shot-putters in track and outstanding punters in football do leave the ground as they throw and punt. Now, though there is no scientific evidence to prove that this is the best method, experience seems to show that these athletes must reduce the vertical forces exerted when they try purposely to stay in contact with the ground.

This is likely to be true in tennis too. If you make a conscious attempt to maintain contact with the ground, you'll probably lose more force than you would be letting yourself leave the ground naturally. Very likely, the jumps we see among good servers are natural results of the combination of forces they apply vertically during their swings. There is good likelihood that the force of the vigorous upward arm swing is transferred to the entire body and so contributes to other forces that cause the server to leaver the ground.

MOVE QUICKLY FOR SPEED

You can apply still another principle of motion to add speed to your serves. Racket speed is increased by increasing the speed of contraction of the muscles used to move it. Now since you alternately bend your arm at the elbow, then straighten it there, the faster you make these motions, the faster your racket will move. It may help if you think of making a "quick pinch" between your upper and lower arm followed by quick and vigorous straightening of that arm. In addition, think of making fast hand, wrist, and forearm action for even more racket speed.

For maximum racket speed, hold your racket loosely during most of your swing but more firmly at impact. There is a positive relationship between ball speed and solid contact. One player was seen to hit two serves in which ball speed differed almost thirty miles per hour, though racket speed was nearly identical. The slower serve was attributed to off-center contact resulting from bad timing and poor racket control, both caused by a loose grip.

SUM YOUR SERVING FORCES

For maximum racket speed, the sources of power described earlier must be timed accurately and applied in proper sequence. Each phase of a stroke should begin before the preceding one stops. When serving, for example, if you straighten your knees much before you begin to straighten your arm at the elbow, you'll have wasted the vertical momentum built up by your leg action. Or, if you delay too long before shifting your weight, you'll have to hurry each subsequent phase of your swing and you'll have less total force as a result.

Scientific movement analysis of good performers shows that the heaviest body parts, those around the mid-section, offer the greatest resistance to the turn in any striking or throwing motion. That's why we see them set in motion first. But the parts lightest in weight—the lower arm and the hand—are the last segments to be moved. When we apply these facts to serving, we can see that your swing will be more efficient when you shift your weight and turn your upper body even as your racket is still moving down into the backscratch position.

But as you practice applying these points of form, check to see that you're not shifting your weight too early. If your body action is spent before your arm and shoulder get into action, you'll be serving at less than maximum force. It's difficult to describe the proper time interval between various phases of the swing except to say that there should be no pause between phases, and that the interval between phases should be long enough to let each phase do its part.

This point of moving the heavier body parts first applies to leg action too. High speed photo analysis of good servers shows that they are straightening their legs (at both the kees and ankles) as their rackets move down behind them into the backscratching position. As a result the upward straightening of the arm comes in as the knees and ankles are completing their tasks. With that timing, that sequence, they are able to sum the forces with which they hit, adding one to another. Try to apply this in your serve if you are looking for a more powerful swing: add one force to another; don't apply them simultaneously. This summation of forces principle (rather than a combination of forces) is applied in all good throwing or hitting motions when speed is an objective.

One way to solve these problems of timing is to experiment to see which sequence provides the best results. Shift your weight sooner and later during your toss; apply upward thrust sooner or later after your toss; and use wrist action and forearm pronation sooner or later in your upswing.

When these motions are timed properly and occur in proper sequence, the total motion is referred to as a kinetic chain. When servers (or baseball pitchers) say they have lost their rhythm, they're admitting either that there is too much slack between links of the chain or that the links follow too quickly one after another. Trial-and-error practice in which you apply conscious thought to adjust the timing and the sequence of your chain should help you find your best serving rhythm.

The same high-speed analysis I mentioned earlier reveals how forces applied to links in the kinetic chain (body segments) operate to produce maximum force. As the forces are added successively, momentum is transferred outward, from the close-in body parts in those farther out. As part of this reaction, the close-in parts slow down. This slowing down may be the result of either centrifugal force or muscular force (positive arm and hand action). Regardless, it is clearly seen in analysis of all good striking and throwing motions. In serves, we see the shoulder slow down as the arm speeds up. Then the arm slows down as the hand speeds up. Lastly, the hand slows down as the racket speeds up.

When the body segments operate this way they act in accordance with a well-known physical law, the Conservation of Angular Momentum. We can see this on a forehand groundstroke, too. As a player turns the hips and shoulders to start a forward swing, the law begins to operate. Momentum is transferred outward from the axis of the turn to the arm causing the hand, at the extremity of the arm, to speed up. As a reaction the arm slows down. Next the momentum of the hand is transferred to the racket, causing it to speed up. And as a consequence, the hand slows down.

This is not to say you should deliberately slow your hand or that you should stop your swing abruptly. Instead, oppose the law and try to increase your hand speed. As you swing for force, slow down gradually in your follow through to avoid strain.

ADJUST THE "LOOK" OF YOUR STROKES

In this chapter, the second of two dealing with mechanics, I listed some mechanical principles that you can apply when hitting for speed. Experiment with them in practice; they may help make your strokes more formidable.

But keep in mind that your strokes should vary depending on the play situation. You may not often want to hit with maximum power. Control instead, may be more important. When it is, you may purposely violate one or another of the power principles mentioned here.

For example, you may often purposely hit from an open stance, knowing that it will restrict your backswing. But when accuracy is more important than speed, the restricted swing may be a better one, a more easily controlled one. This is often true when returning serves.

Adjustment implies flexibility and versatility, which means that you shouldn't ever hope to really "groove" your strokes, to make every forehand look like every other one, for example.

I'm aware that some players and teachers spend a great deal of practice time trying to groove strokes. I believe this is a mistake for this reason: a grooved stroke can be applied only to subsequent shots that occur under identical conditions. This seldom occurs in play. Instead, after making a shot, the next ball you have to swing at is likely to be higher or lower, faster or slower, shorter or deeper than the previous one. And your intended target is likely to be different from the previous one. So let me explain how you may best change your strokes to hit accurately to the various targets.

You must make judgments that enable you to set the variables of the stroke (the slant and angle of your racket; the plane and force of your swing) properly for that next shot. Plainly, if it is to be different, something in your stroke must be different.

Undoubtedly, inner game advocates would dispute this notion that you should evaluate your shots so you can make suitable corrections on succeeding shots. "Don't be judgmental," they say, "Don't criticize yourself."

But a moment's thought should convince you that you can't avoid passing judgment on your performance. Every time you hit the ball you notice whether your shot is good or bad, in or out. And, of course, you keep score which indicates how the majority of your shots compare with those of your opponent, unless you make yourself oblivious to the score.

It isn't very likely, however, that you consider tennis an art form and that you play not to win but merely to experience the joy of movement and for self-expression. More likely, you want to win when you play. Or, at least you want to play well. And, when you're not playing well, you hope to be able to do something about it so you can play better in the future.

In a later chapter I'll describe practice procedures that will help you learn to adjust the variables in your strokes. That kind of practice, in which you apply the mechanical principles discussed here, will require some conscious thought. Which again brings me to the main theme of this book: the most effective way to learn to play is by thinking of how to play. As regards the topic of these last two chapters, the most effective way to build efficient strokes is by knowing what to do and how to do it. This, of course, is contrary to inner game theory and I hold this opinion for good reason—there is no scientific evidence that perfect strokes are already within us just waiting to be discovered. Few, if any, of us have been blessed that way. Most of us have to build our strokes through practice in which we apply conscious thought to our strokes.

SUMMARY. Knowledge of mechanical principles applied in practice can help you hit more aggressively. Changing lever lengths, applying the time-force principle, making use of the law of reaction, summing your forces and motions—these will enable you to hit with a degree of force that is closer to your potential.

CHAPTER 5

FIND YOUR CUES
DURING PRACTICE

OOOOOOOOOOOOOOOOOOOOOOOOOOOOOOOO

In the previous chapters I stressed the importance of practice and of conscious thought during practice. In a few words I say it again here: Think about your strokes during practice so you'll not have to think as much about them during a match.

LIMIT YOUR THINKING

There's a limit to the amount of thinking you or anyone can do while making a particular stroke. Don't clutter your mind with several things to do. Too much thinking may cause you to tighten up and mis-hit. Analysis is necessary. But too much analysis can be disastrous, just as it was for the legendary centipede who coordinated its numerous legs nicely until it tried to figure out exactly how it was done.

In contrast, if you limit your thinking to one simple idea, one that you know works for you, you're more likely to stay relaxed. You can then let the wisdom of your body take over. As I explained in the previous chapter, you'll then be making your stroke at a low level of consciousness and you'll hardly be aware of what you are doing.

Recall my discussion in the first chapter of how this occurs. A tennis stroke is a sensorimotor skill performed as part of a chain reaction of sense organs, brain, and muscles. While preparing to stroke, your eyes send information about the position of the ball to your brain. Meanwhile, your sense organs send information about the position, postures and movements of various parts of your body.

But events during play usually occur too fast for your brain to make much use of all the information being sent to it. Rather, your brain programs a whole series of events in advance. It sends much of the necessary information to the muscles before you actually start your stroke. At least it should. And it can do very little to alter your stroke after it has begun.

How do we know this? From the results of several experiments, two of which I'll describe here.

In one study, done by a group of British sports scientists, several golfers were tested for response time while hitting into a net in a lighted room. All were told that the lights would be turned off at some point in some swings and when they were, the hitter was to stop the swing immediately. The object of the experiment was to find out at what point in the swing the golfer was so committed to it that he couldn't stop it. It was a kind of point-of-no-return test.

None of the golfers tested could stop the swing if the lights went out after a point just barely into the down swing. All could stop it at any point during the backswing.

In another study, this done in our motor development laboratory at the University of California (Berkeley), several subjects were tested for the same reason, but in a test designed differently.

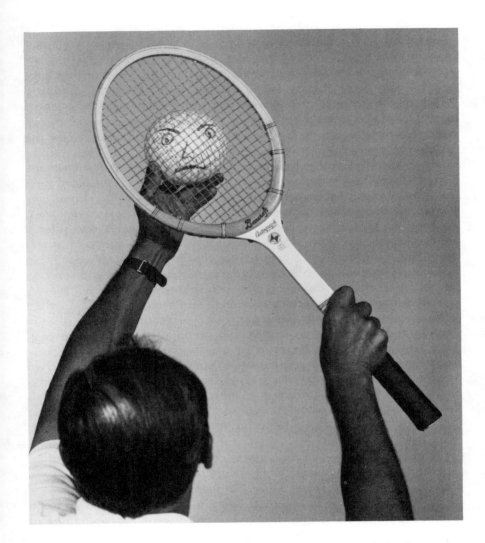

The geometry of impact during a serve is easy to explain. Since the force of your swing always dominates the force of the ball, the direction of the ball's flight off your racket is determined chiefly by the setting of your racket. By imagining a face painted on the ball as shown here, you can apply the simple swing thought, "hit 'em on the nose," to learn to hit more accurately. This can be applied to both a flat serve, in which you flatten the arc of your swing at impact to make your racket move in the same plane it faces, and on a topspin serve, in which you meet the ball before your arm is fully extended so that you can hit the ball with an upward glancing blow. Here, the upward movement of your racket will "lift" the ball a bit while causing it to spin, but the ball will go mainly where your racket faces.

Standing within reach of a string stretched between two poles, each subject took the ready position, with one arm extended horizontally behind him or her to resemble a bowler at the end of the "take away." They were told to swing their arms in pendulum fashion to touch the string in front of them. They were also told that a signal light in front of them may flash at some time during their forward swings. And they were to reverse their swings when they saw the signal.

Here, too, the point-of-no-return was surprisingly early. Not one subject could properly stop or reverse the arm movement if the light went on after he or she started the swing.

The results of these experiments indicate that once you're into a forceful swing, such as a cannon ball serve, it's difficult, and after a certain point impossible, for you to stop it. Your swing may last less than half a second. And since it takes that much time for your brain to receive signals and to order your muscles into action, you can't do much about altering that swing after you've started it.

Fast swings, such as hard serves or drives, may properly be called "ballistic" motions (from the analogy of a projectile: a bullet is set in motion by the explosion and is subject to no additional forces). Similarly, a muscle or a group of muscles contracts to set a body segment in motion. The segment then continues in motion by its own momentum, moving too quickly for the muscle to affect it again. In a sense, the segment outruns the muscle and so the movement is beyond continued muscular control. For this reason slow motion practice of a swing that is intended to be used later as a fast swing may not be realistic.

But to get back to the topic here, I repeat a point I made earlier: you can't guide your fast swings as you make them. About all you can do is start them right and then "let them fly."

But this doesn't mean you must swing out of control. You can and should control your swing. But your control is mainly a matter of aiming your stroke properly and using the right combination of forces—somewhat like aiming a rifle. Specifically, you must set your racket properly, align it properly, and start it in the right direction as regards the line and the plane of your swing. Your success on any particular swing depends on how well you succeed in these tasks.

But even while trying to start your swing properly you can't think of several things at one time. This is why you may have had trouble learning from inexperienced teachers, many of whom make the mistake of trying to teach too many things at once.

In my summer work I constantly caution my assistants about this. And at the university where I have several teachers working under my guidance, I'm equally alert to the problem. You'll understand why by this description of an experience I had several years ago in my club work.

I was sitting with a man, one of our better players, to watch his wife take a lesson from one of my assistants. She wanted to work especially on her backhand, and her husband asked me to watch with him "to see how the lesson goes," to say it in his words.

I was embarrassed about the lesson because for most of it the teacher talked and the student merely stood and listened. When it was finished, she walked over to us and said. "Oh, it was wonderful. I learned so much."

Her husband's reply tells better than I can describe how he (and I) felt about it. "How could you?" he said, "All you did was stand around and listen. You'll probably not be able to change a thing. In fact, you'll probably not even be able to remember anything he said."

Surely you see the point of this story. The woman was given too much instruction and too little action. Her husband knew it and so did I. The teacher would have done a better job had he selected only a point or two that applied to the woman's problem—and if he had helped her practice them *one at a time.*

In contrast to that ineffective lesson, let me tell you of a better one, one that both I as a teacher and you as a learner should remember as a model.

Years ago when I was new at my Colorado resort job, the hotel's golf professional was the late Ed Dudley, internationally known as a player and a teacher.

In the locker room one day I overheard two hotel guests discussing a golf lesson Ed had just given one of them.

"Enjoy your lesson?" said one.

"Oh yes," the other replied, "but all he told me was two things."

"Well," said the first, "are you hitting any better?"

"Oh my yes," came the answer. "I've never hit the ball farther or straighter before. But all he told me was two things, and he didn't say much of anything else. Mostly, he just let me hit a lot of balls."

"If you're hitting so well, what are you complaining about?" said the first man.

"Well, for heaven's sakes, you'd think he'd give more instruction in a half-hour lesson."

I related this incident to Ed to tell him how impressed I was that he helped the man with so little instruction. Ed smiled graciously and said, "Yeh, I remember that fellow, I'm not usually that lucky."

Now, you see, in that lesson Ed succeeded in doing what all of us who teach hope to do in every lesson. He quickly cued in on the man's faults and he offered exactly the right advice with very little talk. He then let the man hit many balls to apply his advice.

Keep this in mind as you practice your strokes. I've said it before, but it's worth saying again: Limit your thinking to one, or at most two, ideas. Put these ideas into the form of something to do—positive thought—rather than something not to do. And select the ideas carefully to make them apply to the particular point of the swing you're working on. As an example, recall my instructions to the woman working on her return of serve. I cued her to raise her racket as the first move in her swing. She concentrated on that one physical act and soon corrected her fault of letting her racket "droop" during her backswing.

You may sometimes be able to think of two things during a swing, but only when those two things are widely spaced, such as at the beginning and at the end of the swing.

Which brings us to the main topic of the rest of this chapter: cues.

CUES

One good way to avoid too much thinking while stroking is by using simple cues. A cue is a word or a group of words, or perhaps a picture or a demonstration, or even a position or a posture, that can be used as a reference pattern for learners to copy and to which they can compare their own performances.

In the remainder of this chapter I'll describe several cues you may use to program your swings. Some are verbal cues, simple and memorable words or phrases that apply either to an entire stroke or to some part of it. Others are visual cues that you see and later may recall through imagery. And still others are tactile: they let you feel what is to be done. And as you would expect, some offer the combined advantages of sight, sound, and feel. In any case, they can all become part of the chain reaction that begins in your brain and ends in muscle movement and a good shot.

CUES FOR THE BACKSWING

Let's start with the same stroke most experienced teachers start their instruction with—the forehand groundstroke. And let's suppose you prefer to make a circular backswing, as most top-flight players do.

For this, visualize a candy-cane suspended in air to the right of you (for a right-handed forehand). "See" the cane lying on its back, with its hook to your right and with its long end slanted up slightly so that it points toward the top of the far fence. Then simply trace the path of the cane as you make your swing. Raise your racket to get it in line with the top of the hook. Lower it through the bottom of the hook and move it upward and forward along the long end of the cane.

For a backhand, visualize the cane on your left side and guide your racket to trace its path. Or you may prefer to use an image that many of my adult students like: visualize a letter "C," one with a long tail extending up toward the far fence, and guide your racket along that path. In other words, cue your stroke through imagery.

But certain body positions and postures may prevent you from making a proper backswing. This is especially true of the position of your shoulders.

On both your forehand and your backhand, if you lower your front shoulder during your backswing you'll tend to raise the racket behind you. As a result it may be too high to permit you to swing up to the ball. If so, learn to keep your shoulders level so that an imaginary line drawn through them would be parallel to the ground. It may even be necessary to *lower* your rear shoulder. This will almost insure your having a low backswing, one low enough to enable you to swing up to meet the ball. John McEnroe strokes this way, with his rear shoulder lowered, on both forehands and backhands. Imitate him, not because he does it but for the same reason he does it; to ensure starting the forward swing at a point below the ball (except when slicing).

I've often helped students make this change in shoulder positions on their forehands by instructing them to point their left hands at the top of the far fence. As they did that, they automatically lowered their right shoulders and their rackets. As a result, they automatically swung up. Try it: it may work for you too.

Swing Along The Line

Having described some cues to use to learn to swing in the proper plane, let me now present cues for learning to guide your racket along the proper line. Or to say it differently, to flatten the arc of your swing.

Recall that in a previous chapter I reminded you that for accurate hitting your racket must be moving straight into the ball along your intended target line. One good way to learn to do this is to use the sidelines and the alleys as target lines.

Stand sideways, on your baseline and two feet away from your right sideline. Make several forehand swings at imaginary balls. On each swing, guide your racket along the sideline as your racket passes through your hitting area, opposite your body. Stretch along the line as far as you can comfortably do so.

After several (or perhaps many) swings, move over to the opposite side of your court and stand sideways alongside your left sideline as if to hit a backhand. Here, too, make several swings, each time guiding your racket along the sideline as far as you can reach.

As you make these swings, be attentive to what you must do physically to swing along the line. You'll see that on the forehand you must turn your body out of the way to let your hitting arm come

BACKHAND: Marty Davis is shown guiding his racket toward his target even in his follow through, the result of having guided it that way through the contact area. Note that his upper body is still sideways to the net. An earlier turn, in which his collar buttons would face the net, could have caused him to pull off the ball, and the result could have been a mis-hit.

through. You'll also have to straighten your arm slightly to allow your racket face to move along the line. Bending your elbow or raising it will cause your racket to move across the line to your left.

On the backhand you'll see that you must handle your body differently to swing along the line. Here, if you turn your shoulders early, as you did for the forehand, you'll pull your racket across the line to your right. So delay your body turn, keeping your shoulders sideways until after you've hit the imaginary ball.

You will notice, too, that you must actually push your racket along the line as you go into your follow-through. If instead, you pull, you'll be making one of the most common faults in the game. As is true of most common faults (and common points of form too) this one has a name, a very descriptive name: It's "pulling off the ball." Avoid this mistake. Pull first, to start your swing. But then push to guide your racket along the target line.

To learn to make these moves properly without much conscious thought of what you are doing, use your collar buttons (or the front zipper on your warm-up jacket) as a reference point, a cue. On your forehands, think of making them face the net immediately as you meet the ball. On your backhands, think of making them face the sideline until *after* you've hit the ball. With these simple thoughts, these cues, you'll not be much concerned about the mechanics of your strokes. Instead, you'll be again relying on the wisdom of the body and as a result your swings will be more efficient.

These subtle differences in body positions are not always fully understood. But they are important regardless of your level of play because they pertain to the fundamental fact of the game: The ball's flight is the resultant of the forces acting on it at impact. One of these forces is the movement of the racket. Make your racket move toward your target as it passes through your hitting area. As I've said before, flatten the arc.

Use Gadgets If Necessary

Besides responding to what you hear and see, you must learn to feel what it is you are doing. Various gimmicks and gadgets can help you here.

For example, when hitting a forehand you shouldn't raise your elbow at impact. Raising it will close the racket face and the result is likely to be an error into the net. Keep your elbow down as you swing, to keep your racket face vertical as if it were standing on edge.

You can learn to feel this proper elbow position by practicing with a ball-can tucked under your arm. Press the can between your hitting arm and your side, midway between your elbow and your arm pit. Make several swings at imaginary balls, keeping the can in place. You'll see that this elbow position virtually ensures a vertical racket face.

CORRECTING A FAULTY VOLLEY: *The author is shown in the first frame demonstrating a common fault on the backhand volley: a raised elbow. The result is almost always a "pop up," as shown here. In the second frame he is shown using the can under his arm to correct the fault. A practice partner feeds balls to him to let him catch the feeling of his proper elbow position.*

All-American collegian Larry Stefanki shows good form (good adjustment) on a tight backhand volley. He has avoided the common fault of pulling off the ball (pulling to his right) by extending his arm through the contact area to make his racket move toward his target.

After several swings, remove the can. On succeeding swings make your arm feel as if you're still pressing a can under it. And when you're actually hitting a ball, make your arm feel that way too. You'll probably make more solid contact as a result. In other words, recall the feeling and use it as a cue.

I recall using this procedure recently to correct a youngster's raised elbow. After our lesson he wandered into my shop and noticed a photo of Jimmy Connors on a magazine cover. Connors was shown making solid contact on a forehand groundstroke, with his elbow down exactly as we had practiced a few moments earlier.

While discussing this photo, I used a felt pen to sketch a ball under Connor's arm, making it look as if he too had been instructed with this can (or ball)-under-the-arm procedure. I then tore the cover from the magazine and gave it to the boy so he could use it to remember the point of our lesson. Needless to say, with such strong reinforcement he soon learned to keep his elbow down during his forehand stroke.

The expression "leading with the elbow" describes a common fault on the backhand. If you're having trouble generating force in your swing, you may be making this mistake. Check to see that your forearm and your hitting hand are where they should be as you start your forward swing: your arm pressed against your mid section and your hand pressed against your rear hip. If, instead, your elbow protrudes away from your body toward the net, you'll have a tendency to poke at the ball. The result is likely to be a weak shot.

You can correct this poking action by pressing the can (or a ball) against your stomach with your hitting forearm during your backswing. With your arm close to your body this way, you're more likely to make a forceful swing at the ball. The result is more likely to be a long, smooth stroke, one that provides more force than does a short poke.

If the can (or ball)-against-your-body routine is too awkward for you to use, you can learn the proper arm action on the backhand by using your elbow as a physical cue.

As the ball approaches, bend your arm at the elbow so that you can point your forearm at the ball. You may prefer to think of this as "pointing your elbow at the ball." If so, the result will be the same; a bent arm backswing. But to avoid the fault of leading with your elbow, make certain your hitting hand is close to your left side. With your arm bent at the elbow, you'll be able to straighten it forcefully as you move your upper arm at your shoulder to start your forward swing. This combination of arm and elbow action is likely to give you a more forceful swing than would a straight-armed swing.

Adjust For Placement

Though I've just suggested that your arm be straight at impact on your backhands, it can't always be so. In fast play when you can't always be set to hit at arm's length from the ball you'll have to hit with a slightly bent arm. But then, by straightening your arm in the follow-through, you can flatten the arc of your swing and avoid the fault of pulling off the ball.

You may also purposely hit backhands with a bent arm for a second reason: to place your shot accurately. Here, instead of adjusting your wrist to make your racket face properly (as I suggested for the forehand), adjust the position of your elbow. To hit the ball to your left, for example, meet the ball with a slightly bent arm, before it has straightened. To hit to your right, meet the ball after your arm has straightened.

I find it often helps students when I remind them of the difference here between forehands and backhands. That distinction may have significance for you too. On the forehand, place the ball by making wrist adjustments. On the backhand, make elbow adjustments. Actually, what you'll be doing is meeting the ball sooner or later (in terms of its flight toward you). But you'll probably find this easier to do by thinking of making these adjustments rather than thinking of changing the timing of your total swing.

I've been successfully teaching placement in this way (rather than the conventional way) ever since an experience I had at my club years ago. While teaching a woman who had trouble controlling her shots, I asked her to adjust her stance and her timing while using identical form, i.e., no change in wrist or elbow positions. She stopped me in my tracks, however, by asking how much difference in timing is necessary. I explained it was only a matter of inches, of fractions of a second. She then asked how fast her husband's serves travelled. When I explained that we had timed them at close to one-hundred miles an hour, she replied, "This is ridiculous. I can't even time my swing right to hit slow balls straight ahead and now you're asking me to adjust my swing to only fractions of a second when balls are coming that fast. Ridiculous," she said again.

Her response to that conventional method for placing the ball prompted me to devise the method I've described here: physical adjustments at the wrist and elbow. It helps my students hit accurately. I'm confident that it will work for you too.

Cues For The Serve

Most experienced teachers have devised clever bits of imagery to teach the serve. One of the most effective of these originated with the late Jean Hoxie, a teaching friend of mine from Hamtramck, Michigan. She had her young students pretend their racket was a vehicle, a bike or an auto, moving along a roadway. They were told to think of moving their rackets "down a hill, up a hill, over a bridge and finally home." As silly as this may sound, it worked for most of her students, many of whom were nationally ranked and were especially good servers. Try it; it may work for you too.

I have always believed that the more descriptive and realistic cues are, the more impact they make. For this reason I teach the full serve motion by demonstrating while describing exactly what I'm doing. But I use simple terms.

For example, I show and have my students imitate the starting (and aiming) position; from that posture we trace the racket's path. It flows down past the *knee*, then rises up behind us to point toward the top of the rear *fence*. At that instant the upper body begins to turn toward the net as the racket is lowered behind the *back*. From that point the racket is flung diagonally upward into the *ball*.

Several (or sometimes many) practice swings are then made at imaginary balls. In each swing the check points are stated either softly or aloud, depending on the circumstances: it's KNEE, FENCE, BACK, BALL. In keeping with my theory of flexibility and permissive instruction, I permit slight variations in serve swings provided they resemble to a reasonable degree the full path I've described here.

If you're uncertain about your serve, if it doesn't feel right, and if you are afraid it doesn't resemble the serves you see in top-flight tennis, try this knee-fence-back-ball routine. Repeat the check points aloud if necessary (or to yourself, to save embarrassment) as your racket moves into each position. After you feel you've learned the swing, try it with the ball. Toss the ball on the "fence" part of your swing and shift your weight on to your front foot as you toss. Turn your shoulders counterclockwise to start your forward swing as your racket points toward the top of the rear fence. If you toss accurately as high as you can place the center of your strings and slightly in front of your right shoulder, you're likely to develop a smooth, well-coordinated swing, with the important links of your kinetic chain getting into action properly, one after another.

PLACING THE BALL: This volleyer makes adjustments with his wrist to place his forehand shot. In Frame A, a straight wrist enables him to place his shot to his left. In Frame B, the laid-back wrist lets him meet the ball later and he can thus steer it off to the right. Frames C and D show elbow adjustments that enable him to change the direction of his shots on the backhand volley. The elbow close to his body permits him to hit to his right. The elbow out away from his body permits him to steer the ball to his left. The same kinds of adjustments can be made when hitting groundstrokes. ▷

(A)

(B)

(C)

(D)

Adjusting For Placing The Serve

But swinging properly doesn't guarantee that you'll make a good serve. You must also hit the ball properly, making contact at the right place on the ball while your racket is moving in the right direction. For this there's a helpful gadget that provides reference points for you.

Use a felt marking pen and paint a face on a ball. Hold the ball up above your head as if the face is looking directly over your head toward the rear fence. Place your racket strings against the nose of the face to see and to feel the proper wrist and racket positions at contact.

In your serve practice, visualize and imagine this face on the ball every time you swing at it. If you intend to hit a flat serve your racket must be moving straight toward your target area (your opponent's court) and it must meet the ball squarely on the nose. But if you intend to hit with topspin, you must hit the ball a glancing blow. For this, your racket must be moving up and across the ball at impact, hitting it on the nose *while* moving toward the left eye of the imaginary face. Your cues for programming this kind of swing may be, "swing up and across the ball," or perhaps, "hit nose to eye."

You can use the imaginary face on the ball to correct each previous service fault. If a serve goes into the net, it's probably because you made contact on the forehead of the face. If a serve goes too long, it's probably because you made contact on the chin. As you see either of these faults occur, plan to correct your next swing, the second of your two allotted serves. Adjust your swing, especially the timing of your wrist action, to place your racket on the nose. Your program cue? "Hit 'em on the nose."

But you may mistakenly place your racket either too high or too low on the ball for another reason: bad placement of your toss.

If you toss the ball too far forward, you will almost certainly meet the ball after your arm has reached full extension. As a result you will make contact toward the top of the ball rather than on the nose. If you toss back too far you will probably meet the ball on the upward part of your swing rather than at the high point of your arc, as you should. As a result, you will almost certainly make contact too low on the ball.

You can correct your inaccurate tosses by using the fence as a gimmick. Stand about two feet away from one of the vertical posts, facing it as if you are going to serve toward it. Start a service swing and toss the ball vertically in line with the post, stopping your swing when your racket is in the back-scratching position. Use the fence post as a guide and toss so that your ball travels upward alongside it, close to it but not touching it. Repeat this half-swing and toss as often as necessary to learn to toss accurately, vertically from your release point.

Cues For Ball Control

The imaginary face on the ball you use for serving can help you learn to control the up-and-down flight of the ball on your groundstrokes too. For those shots again visualize a face on the ball and as you swing, try to hit the face on the nose. Here, too, you have instant feedback: your shot was either too high or too low. A netted shot usually means your racket face was closed at impact. With the face on the ball, you can imagine that you hit on the hairline. In contrast, a shot long at the baseline usually means you hit on the chin of the face. Being attentive to these results, these consequences, of your shots can help you learn to adjust your racket face on succeeding shots. Eventually, with sufficient practice, you'll learn to set your racket properly more often.

Cues For The Volleys

Two simple bits of imagery may help you volley better almost immediately. They often work that quickly for my students.

For a forehand volley, recall the childhood game of patty-cake. Pretend you're playing patty-cake against the ball. As it approaches, simply raise your racket to place it against the ball just as you raised your hand to press it against a friend's hand in that game. You'll seldom need to do much more than that when the ball is within reach and above your waist.

Another analogy can be equally effective when used during a backhand volley. If you're having trouble with that shot, try this. Visualize a man standing at attention to honor the flag, with his hand across his chest. Imitate him, placing your racket across your chest and shoulder. While in that posture, have a partner feed balls to you, aiming at your racket face. Move your racket as little as necessary to place it behind the ball. Move it to your left or right, up or down. And move it forward—toward the oncoming ball—with only that slight amount of force necessary to attain the speed you want on your shot. Practice the volleyer's salute. Many backhand volleys can be hit as simply as that.

Cues For The Smash

The two most common mistakes made when smashing are overswinging and improper positioning. It's easy to understand why most inexperienced players swing too much when smashing: They've been told to use their serve swing. Yet even casual observation of good smashers in action reveals that most of them use a shorter, more controlled swing than they do when serving. Specifically, most of them carry the racket back past their right ear (rather than past the right knee as when serving). From that high position, it is then lowered behind the back during the hitting motion.

A simple way to learn this kind of swing is by relating it to your forehand volley rather than to your serve. I've had much success using this analogy and I'm certain it will work for you too.

Have a practice partner feed soft, high balls to you so you can *volley* them away for winners. Ask him or her to gradually hit higher and higher (but not yet a full-length, full-height lob), so that you have to reach upward fully to place your racket on the ball. In all of these strokes, use your volley-like preparatory swing, moving your racket up past your ear as you take it back.

As your feeder's shots get still higher, you will probably have to move to get properly in position to hit. And with these higher shots, these low lobs, you'll have time to pause between your backswing and your hitting motion. Pause with your racket pointing up behind you, not dangling loosely behind your back. You'll have to hold the racket firmly to keep it up behind you, and that firm grip will give you better control than would a loose one.

To avoid the second fault I've mentioned, move carefully to get into the proper hitting location. Use several little steps and expect that you'll have to move until the last split-second before you start your swing. Bad positioning results from either careless movement or misjudgement. This latter mistake results from making the judgement decisions too early, too confidently. Always assume that you may be wrong in your early judgement of where to move and of how fast to move. To say it differently, don't set yourself early and then wait for the ball. Instead, be moving while you're waiting, even if only to raise and lower your heels. In this way, you'll be more ready to make last-second adjustments in position, in location, to correct early misjudgements.

Reviewing this chapter, you'll agree that I've described how you might use cues not only to build the "look" of your swing but also to control the flight of the ball. I believe this last point of stroking (racket control and its result on ball control) is often overlooked in tennis instruction. For example, I recently saw a half-hour television demonstration of serving during which time not one word was said about controlling the up-and-down flight of the ball. Don't make this mistake in your practice. Remember—the ball goes mainly where your racket faces. Use the face on the ball to help place your racket on it properly.

Admittedly, you're not likely to always get immediate and startling results with the cues, images, and picture words I describe and recommend in this book. But you are likely to hit better over a period of time. Experiment with them. And experiment to find cues of your own too. Search for meaningful words, colorful phrases and expressions that help you understand what you are to do. You're likely to hit better sooner than if you practice aimlessly without conscious thought, hoping that something good will happen. With the proper use of cues, you can make it happen, in both practice as I described here, and in play, as I describe in the following chapter.

SUMMARY. Don't try to think of several things while practicing strokes. Instead, find one, or at most two, swing thoughts to work on. Use simple cues, picture words, gimmicks, gadgets, or other devices to learn to set body segments into correct positions and/or to move them properly. With the proper use of these devices—and with conscious thought—you can learn to hit better sooner than if you practice aimlessly while waiting for good performance to emerge naturally.

CHAPTER **6**

Use Your Cues
During Play

OOOOOOOOOOOOOOOOOOOOOOOOOOOOOOOOOOOOOO

My explanation in the previous chapter of how you can use cues in practice leads logically to the question of how useful they can be during serious play. A year or so ago I noticed an incident in World Team Tennis competition that clearly answers that question.

Vitas Gerulaitis, then rated the fifth best player in the world, was playing Sandy Mayer of the well-known brother combination. Near the end of the close, hard-fought match, I noticed Fred Stolle, Gerulaitis' coach, offering advice to him from his position on the sideline while he was preparing to serve. Frequently after good serves Gerulaitis gave Stolle the thumb-and-forefinger "OK" sign, apparently to signify that his advice was having a positive effect.

Being curious to know what Stolle was saying, I moved down several rows of seats to be close enough to hear. To my surprise, Stolle was telling Gerulaitis simply to "hit up, hit up."

Hearing Stolle's instructions, I remembered that he had written earlier about his coaching Gerulaitis to improve his serve and that he was correcting a tendency to hit with a slightly bent arm. More likely than not, it was Gerulaitis' way of responding to mental pressure on crucial points. He inadvertently restricted the force of his swing and was too anxious to see the result. Consequently, his arm was not fully extended at impact and the result was often a weak, netted shot.

Stolle went on to explain that he was having Gerulaitis swing all out by emphasizing the upward motion of the swing. In keeping with sound mechanics, an upward swing with a fully extended arm is preferred over a bent-arm swing with its resultant "pushy" motion. Here, apparently, Gerulaitis and Stolle were able to correct that fault in practice *and* in play with the simple cue to hit up on the ball.

The same simple procedure that worked for Gerulaitis will probably work for you, too. In practice find a useful cue. Use that same cue in play to help reproduce the stroke you learned in practice.

At the risk of laboring the point, consider this incident from the sport of basketball.

In an important tournament game played in San Francisco this past season, a player won the game for his team by making two free throws after time had run out. (He was fouled while in the act of shooting just as the final gun went off.) Afterward, newspaper reporters swarmed around him and asked the usual questions. "Weren't you nervous? What were you thinking about as you prepared to shoot those free throws?"

"Naw," he replied, "coach reminded me to follow through real long and smooth, and that's what I was thinking to do. Lucky for me, it worked. It always does in practice."

I hope you'll agree that the procedures used by both players in these tennis and basketball incidents are antithetical to inner game theory. But let's consider: could relaxing and simply letting things happen have worked any better? Or as well? I hardly think so.

Let me state the point of these incidents plainly because it's the main point of this chapter. The same cues you use in practice to build and to improve your strokes may help you reproduce those strokes in play.

I say "may" here because possibly you're already playing at a level that precludes your using a great deal of conscious thought on strokes. If you're not at that level, if you haven't yet developed confidence in your strokes, you'll benefit from thinking about them in the way I describe in this chapter.

You may understand this apparent contradiction better if you understand one major premise on which my teaching is based and on which this book is written. I believe that players play differently—and think differently—at various levels of development. Not only do they differ obviously in strokes and shots and tactics and strategy. They also differ in what they think about.

For example, a player who is still building strokes thinks about certain specific things that have to do with the mechanics of strokes. But a player who has already developed good strokes need think only about a certain cue or a gimmick or a gadget that worked in practice, as Gerulaitis did.

Spend a few moments thinking about your game to determine your present level of development. Rate your playing ability. Then decide whether the majority of your time on the court should be spent in rallying or in competitive play. For the remainder of this chapter I'll assume that you're beyond the first level of development and are ready to learn to use cues in actual play.

I've suggested that you practice to learn to cue yourself to perform in some specific way—to lower your elbow, or to tighten your grip, or to straighten your arm, or whatever. But regardless of how hard you practice, regardless of how often you repeat that point of form, there's no guarantee that you'll always be able to do it in play.

Our minds function differently during serious, competitive tennis. We usually feel psychological pressure to win, or to do well, or to at least look good. And this is true of all of us regardless of our levels of play.

A moment's thought should convince you that the pressure you feel in match play is simply the fear of missing. And the solution is just as plain: occupy your mind with something other than the fear of missing.

The simplest way to do this is to have a suitable cue, a positive thought, in mind as you begin your stroke. It may be the same cue you think of during practice. Or it may be a different one. Regardless of which you use, occupy your mind with the cue to block out negative thoughts (the fear of missing, remember?) and to let yourself go about the business of stroking at a low level of consciousness.

FIND YOUR ANTI-CHOKE DEVICES

One good way to establish cues is to analyze what you're doing when you're playing well. We all have days when things just seem to go right. No double faults, few unforced errors, many good passing shots—we all have so few of those days that we should be certain to make the best of them.

On those "good" days, take a moment to analyze an exceptionally good shot immediately after you make it. Try to catch the feeling of it. Put it in words and describe it to yourself. And as soon afterwards as you can, write it down for future reference. When a bad day comes along you'll have these to fall back on and perhaps be able to get your game back on track.

Your cues may be more useful to you if you regard them as "anti-choke" devices. With that terminology, that descriptive name, you're more likely to recall them and to use them in pressure situations where you normally tighten up.

Let me give some examples of how I've helped students find their own anti-choke devices.

I'm sure you'll agree that having to serve the second ball on a crucial point is a choke situation. Though the serve action appears simple enough to reproduce time and time again, when serving at

Many inner problems are caused by outer faults. To correct the fault of being too wristy, press your racket against the net band as shown here. As you begin to catch the feeling of the firm, laid-back wrist position, swing at the band, smacking your racket face fully into it. After several swings, swing above the net, barely missing it, while keeping your wrist firmly laid back, as when you hit the band. Finally, practice hitting balls with this same wrist position. Later, in serious play, recall this feeling and use the swing thought as an anti-choke device.

add-out in a critical game in an important match, self-doubts often arise.

To prevent this from happening to my students, I ask them to describe certain feelings they've had when serving well. And since I try in my instruction to use picture words that convey a vivid mental image, I am often able to get my students to describe their serves that way. I then suggest that they recall those words, that image, when preparing to serve. This procedure helps many of them stay loose, as we say, and as a result their serves are more effective. If you're not already doing it, this procedure may work for you, too.

Surely you've heard the often used verbal cue that describes the service motion as "throwing a ball." I use that expression regularly in my teaching because most learners who have had previous throwing experience usually learn to swing properly when they make that analogy.

By changing that expression you can make it apply to the entire serve action. You can then program yourself to do as it suggests and so use it as an anti-choke device.

As you take your stance to serve, tell yourself each time how easy it is. All you have to do is throw the ball up and then "throw" your racket at the ball. Recite this softly to yourself each time you prepare to serve, especially in pressure situations. Here you may be so busy talking to yourself that you'll not have time to worry about missing.

MAKE CONSCIOUS CORRECTIONS

Different problems require different cues. For example, I recall that a woman came into my tennis shop to ask for a few words of advice. She complained that her serves weren't going in on that day, yet on the preceding day "she didn't have that trouble," to quote her. I went out to a court for only a few minutes to watch her serve. Sure enough, most of them were going into the net. "See," she said, "that's what happens. Why do they all go down too much? It wasn't that way yesterday."

Now before I explain how we solved her problem let me explain that different performances, different results, on successive and/or alternate days are not unusual in tennis or in any sport. For example, Tom Watson, the golf champion, has said that the body changes, that it is different each day and that, consequently, each shot requires constant reminders for setting up and for swinging. You recognize this as more anti-inner game theory; of course, this time it's from one of the world's best golfers.

Now getting back to the woman server, I found out that she couldn't explain simply and technically why the ball goes where it goes. I hope you are anticipating my explanation here because I've said it before. I repeat myself for emphasis because it's so important: The ball goes mainly where the racket faces.

To make a strong visual impact on her I used a large orange ball with facial features painted on it as I explained in the previous chapter. I held the ball above her head so that the face on it appeared to be looking directly over her head. I then showed her how she could place her racket on the mouth, the nose, or the head of the face merely by changing the position of her wrist while the racket is extended up toward the ball. I then had her swing slowly so she could adjust the timing of that wrist action to place the ball on the nose of the face.

I then explained that on each point she has two tries to get one serve in. I explained that she has instant feed-back; she sees her serve go into the net or too long. I suggested that she conclude from what she sees how accurately she placed the racket on the ball. Having given her that information while I was demonstrating and while she was imitating, I let her serve. Truly, in only eight or ten minutes she was almost always able to serve a ball in after having missed the preceding one. In other words, no double faults.

The next step, of course, was to encourage her to do that same kind of head work and wrist work in play that was so effective for her in practice. Weeks later while she was telling me how well she was serving she also explained that she is so busy thinking about those things that she doesn't have time to worry about missing.

I consider that incident a perfect example of how players benefit from thinking during play. And as it works in tennis so does thinking work in other sports. Golfer Jack Nicklaus, for example, says he always thinks before he hits the ball. He says that when he loses form, he tries to determine why by analyzing the cause and effect relationships that occur during his swing. He then tries to make the necessary changes in his stroke. Surely you can see that I was asking the woman server mentioned earlier to use a similar procedure to correct her faults.

The matter of using the wrist when serving needs some elaboration here. Recently we in tennis have been hearing that there is no wrist action in the serving motion; that pronation of the lower arm provides most of the racket momentum. I feel strongly that teachers who say so are in error. Admittedly, inward rotation, pronation, and extension of the arm do provide a great deal of racket speed. But wrist action applied along with these actions provides even more speed.

I say this because of the results of EMG experiments conducted at our University of California (Berkeley) motor development laboratory. There, I and several other players served with electrodes attached to our wrist extensors and flexors. We saw clear indications of these muscles being activated as we served. And the timing was just as one would imagine it to be: extension before impact and flexion later but still before and during impact.

Encouraged by the results of our experiments, I've helped many students increase the speed of their serves by suggesting they use a butt-in-the-palm grip. In almost every one of my groups of 15-20 students, two or three of them serve faster (as measured by our radar speed gun) immediately after being shown this grip variation. If you've never tried it, it's worth experimenting with.

After placing your hand on the racket handle in your normal serve grip, slide your hand down the handle until the butt is in your palm. With that "long" grip, you'll not be able to squeeze your last two fingers around the handle. Now if you'll recall my earlier discussion of the relationship between grip firmness and wrist action, you'll understand why you can get more wrist action with such a grip. Earlier, in my discussion of ground strokes, I suggested you hold a firm grip to have a firm wrist. When serving, however, you'll be better off with a loose wrist. And so you should hold a loose grip.

PROGRAM YOUR SWING

One of my most useful devices for helping students overcome the fear of missing when serving is the knee-fence-back-ball routine I described in the preceding chapter. I encourage my students to use that routine in play just as we used it when they were learning to serve. I want them to call out audibly (but softly, of course) the four check points as they move their rackets through those points.

I know this procedure works for many of my students. They tell me they pretend they are back in their early lessons and they produce the swing in response to those cues just as they learned to do earlier. But at this stage in their development, they are also able to place the racket on the ball properly at least once in every two tries and so they avoid double faults. Like the basketball player I described earlier, they find that this routine, these cues, work for them in practice and so they expect them to work in play. In that positive frame of mind, they are more likely to serve better on crucial points.

You may find that you have to dispense with your customary ball-bouncing ritual to talk to yourself this way. If so, well and good. Bouncing the ball four, five or six times is only a mannerism. But tossing properly and swinging properly are essential points of form. I'm sure you'll agree that it makes sense to let points of form take precedence over a questionable mannerism.

If you're having trouble tossing accurately, this gimmick may help you. As you take your serving position, look at the far fence and select a fence post that is in line with where you want your toss to be.

Then, as you toss, guide your hand (and the ball) upward in line with the post. Release the ball at face height as you normally do.

This gimmick often works for my students immediately after I have them first practice tossing up a post while standing only a foot or two away from it, as I described in the previous chapter. Then of course, they don't complete their swings; they stop after having made the toss.

There may be an even better way for you to improve your toss: Simply watch yourself make it. Look at your tossing hand as you toss; don't look up to where you intend to place the ball. Look at the ball in your hand for the full length of your tossing motion. After releasing the ball, continue to watch it until your racket makes contact.

I'm aware that most good players look up at the sky and then toss to where they're looking. But some very good players, among them Jimmy Connors, look at their tossing hands instead. Try it; it may work for you, too.

You may develop better control of your arm by guiding it up a post or by watching your hand. But the real value of these gimmicks may be that each keeps you so busy doing something that you don't have time to worry about serving a fault.

For another example of serve cues, one lady describes her toss this way: "I carry the ball up and release it *gently*." A man says, "I bend my wrist back and use my hand as a launching platform."

You see that these two players have different images of their toss. One tosses gently; the other *launches* the ball, which implies a more vigorous motion. Both players have learned to focus their attention on their particular image as they toss. As a result, they seldom tighten up and toss badly.

Now, at this point you may be thinking that all this is easier said than done. True, but it is not hard to do if you practice doing it. It's a matter of marshalling your thoughts, and then doing it.

In keeping with the computer analogy made earlier, we can describe this procedure as "programming" your swing. Programming increases the probability of doing at least one part of the swing correctly. The result is more likely to be a correct swing.

But you need not limit your programming to only the start of your swing. I know a woman who has successfully programmed herself to think of "peeling the skin off the ball" to apply spin to it on her serve. And, a man I teach thinks of straightening his arm vigorously as he hits flat serves as Gerulaitis learned to do. As he explains it—"I can't very well hold back (choke) while I'm snapping my arm straight." And still another man thinks of jumping into his serve. He explains it as an all-or-none proposition, saying, "I think of jumping as hard as I can. The rest of my serve just seems to follow." More anti-choke devices, don't you agree?

KEEP IT SIMPLE

When you practice and then play for practice to discover suitable cues, try to coin expressions that convey the image or the feel or the purpose of the total movement. If possible, express them in the form of axioms or in some kind of easy-to-remember phrases. The well-known golfing axiom, "never up, never in," is a good example. Many golfers apply this on the greens to keep from putting short, the idea being that they can't hit the ball into the cup unless they hit it as far as the cup.

An example in tennis comes from a woman student who tends to hit her backhand into the net after rallying for five or six good shots. She's learned to remind herself to first hit the ball over the net in order to hit it in. For this, she cues herself with the expression "up and over" and she emphasizes the first word as she repeats that expression to herself as she strokes.

There's a lot of wisdom in that device for two reasons. A well-known statistic in the game tells us that the large majority of points are lost on errors, (not won on good shots). Obviously, then, any plan that helps her keep the ball in play is a good one.

Secondly, my own personal observation leads me to conclude that average learners err by hitting into the net rather than by hitting too long or too wide. And so any plan that helps her avoid those frequent errors is a good one. Remember: never over, never in.

One of the best examples I've seen of how thinking players can make cues work for them in play occurred during one of my club's invitational mixed doubles tournaments.

Late one afternoon, after the day's matches had been completed, a husband-and-wife team from out of town began to practice for the next day's match. As I watched I noticed they were practicing specifically to improve the woman's net game. She stood at the net, where she would stand in play if her partner were serving. He stood across the court from her, at the baseline, where he would stand in play to return that same serve. From his location he hit balls in her direction while at the same time offering advice.

The man knew the game well, having had top-flight college experience, and so his advice was sound. Except for one thing. As he prepared to make his shots he had to watch the ball, naturally. And so he couldn't see a mistake his wife was making at that instant, as his racket met the ball.

Strangely, in anticipation of the ball coming to her she lowered her racket by extending her arms at the elbows. She then had to raise her racket quickly as part of her backswing. As a result of that lowered

Ivan Lendl is shown volleying into the alley (in a doubles match) against a crosscourt return from an opponent. On these kinds of shots you must be aware of the geometry of impact. If you merely block the shot (as is usually the case on close-in volleys), the ball will deflect off your racket at an angle almost equal to the angle at which it approached your racket. (The angle of incidence [almost] equals the angle of deflection; friction and elasticity between the ball and the strings alters it somewhat.) To hit accurately you must make your racket face midway between the angle formed by the ball's line of approach and your intended target line. Think of it as "cutting the angle in half." If instead you make your racket face directly toward your target, you're likely to hit wider than you intended.

racket and that extra motion to her swing, she mis-hit many balls and even became fearful of getting hurt.

When I explained to her husband that he couldn't see what she was doing, he asked me to feed balls to her so he could watch her. He quickly agreed with my diagnosis and began to instruct her to correct that fault. His advice was simple: "Keep your racket up. That's it: racket up," and so on.

A year later that couple again came to our tournament. This time they reached the finals, and as club professional, I had the honor of umpiring their final match. From my chair position, close to and alongside a sideline, I could hear most of what the players were saying to one another. To my pleasant surprise, the husband-and-wife team put to use the volley instruction we were involved with a year ago. They told me later that they had practiced it regularly since that time.

When the man served, his wife took a position very close to the net, so close that the receivers couldn't possibly place their returns to her feet. In other words, all balls hit to her were played as high volleys.

But almost always, just before serving the man reminded her to hold her racket up and to block the ball. I made a point to notice how well she followed his advice. She did so perfectly. In her ready posture her racket head was almost head high. That was higher than necessary but it enabled her to simply block the oncoming balls. From that location and with that new technique the woman was able to handle almost all returns made to her.

No one can explain better than this woman how this combination of head work and racket work made her a better volleyer. "It's easy," she said, "as long as I remember to hold my racket up. And when I play with Tom he doesn't let me forget to."

Again I say, inner-game theory would not have, could not have, worked any better. Thinking pays off. In this case she thought of the simple cue of raising the racket.

ALLITERATION MAY HELP

A personal observation of mine may help you find useful cues for your own game. I've found that alliterated expressions tend to have a stronger effect on students than do ordinary ones. They are more likely to bring out the proper response.

I'm reminded of a recent experience in which I helped a student use alliterated cues effectively. A woman in one of my school classes asked for my help in learning to hit with more speed. As I watched her I noticed that her wrist was loose as she hit on both forehands and backhands. When I pointed this out to her and explained that she was losing speed through racket recoil because of her loose grip and loose wrist (I've already explained how these are related), she explained that she had been taught to hit that way, "to let the racket head do the work," as she put it.

Now, merely by holding her racket firmly at impact she immediately hit harder. She was elated with the results. But she'd usually remember to do it properly for only two or three successive hits and then revert back to her loose wrist method. Plainly, we needed a more vivid cue.

Luckily for both of us, I remembered a teaching point I've used before: the finish of the stroke is the one part of the stroke the hitter can see. So I asked her to *look at* her finish each time to see that she was firm there, the logic being that if she's firm at the finish she'd probably be firm at the hit.

This worked immediately too, and though it seems like a repetition of a previous cue, it was just different enough to catch and maintain her interest. We were able to describe her swing as having a firm finish, but she preferred to put it into her own words and cued herself by thinking of "finishing firmly."

When I saw her a week or so later and asked how her power strokes were going, she replied, "Real good, as long as I see myself finish firmly." I have no doubt that she'll soon learn to end her stroke that way habitually while not having to look to see that she finishes properly.

A woman student of mine reduces tension when serving by thinking of hitting "nicely on the nose." And a man I know controls his wrist action on groundstrokes by remembering to be *flexible*, then *firm*.

And still another student, a woman, improved her volleys considerably by learning to *squeeze* her grip to *stop* her racket at impact. By recalling this simple alliterated phrase during her volley practice, she learned to restrict her stroke (from the long swing she used previously) to make it more like the conventional punching motion used when volleying. I tried using that word, "punching," with her first. Her reply embarrassed me because I could see the word was not appropriate for her. "I can't remember ever having punched anyone," she said. Needless to say, I've been careful about using that cue ever since.

Another woman came to me for lessons complaining that her serve felt "disjointed" when she tried to guide her racket through reference points she had been shown. And when she demonstrated to me, indeed it did look that way, as if she were swinging by-the-numbers, so to speak.

To correct this I suggested that she ignore the check points and that she merely let her racket *flow* down and then *fling* it at the ball. I condensed this instruction to, "Let if flow, then fling it." She immediately began to swing smoothly, with less effort and with more force. The result was a better serve, almost instantly.

Among several other alliterated expressions that I've used successfully are the following:

"Adjust the angle." This remark is often helpful to players who miss successive shots because of inaccurate racket setting.

For example, a man in one of my school classes netted four balls in a row. This occurred in pre-class practice before I had gotten the class into my usual instruction on adjusting the variables. (Recall that one of the variables to be adjusted is the setting of the racket face.) As I approached him and before I could say anything he asked, "Why do all my shots go into the net?" and, "How can I correct that?".

With as few words as possible, I explained that he must make his hitting surface slant upward slightly to hit the ball up and over the net. I then stood behind him and placed my hand over his and together we hit several dropped balls. I showed him that a simple clockwise turning motion of the forearm would let him open the racket face. With my help he saw it, he felt it, and he did it. He adjusted the angle of the racket face to correct netted balls. We agreed to use that expression, "adjust the angle," to prompt him to make a conscious correction after those kinds of misses. This anti-inner game instruction worked so well that I've used it many times since, almost always with good results.

"Make some wrinkles in the wrist." A common fault among inexperienced players is loosening the grip and wrist when hitting low backhands. As a result, they lose control of the racket, and often mis-hit the ball. As a corrective device I ask them to cock the wrist slightly, as I explained in a previous chapter. To be more specific, I suggest you cock your wrist just enough to cause some wrinkles to form at the back of it. With the wrist in that position, you'll be able to hold the racket more firmly and as a result you'll have better control of it.

"Run softly, then stop." Eye specialists tell us that when the head is moving while the eyes try to track a moving ball, the eyes don't fixate on the ball too well. As a result, vision is blurred slightly. For this reason I ask students to move as little as possible during a stroke, and especially to avoid hitting while in the middle of a step. I also ask them to set their feet down softly as they make the last steps before swinging.

I explain that running softly is a lot like walking on thin ice that may break under their weight. It's simply a matter of using the leg muscles to set each foot down softly. Running with bent knees and while leaning forward more than is customary make it easier to set the feet down softly too. These changes in running form are worth the effort they'll take you to learn them. They make the head steady. As a result you're likely to make a more accurate judgment of the ball's speed and position.

"Step for the ball, don't stretch for it." This clue is used for the same reason as the previous one; to help learners get into a good hitting position. Many inexperienced players stop too far from the ball, then have to stretch to reach it. Often this mistake occurs because they step in the wrong direction with the left foot for forehands as they start their swings. By encouraging them to step rather than stretch they are usually able to position themselves nicely alongside the ball. When they do, the result is usually a more accurate shot. Remember this as you move to get into position to hit. Adjust your last step carefully so you'll be comfortably in position to hit it. Step, don't stretch to reach the ball.

"Hit the hell out of it." One student who tended to hold back and hit too softly when he should have been hitting all out, cued himself to overcome that tendency with this expression. He taught himself to say this to himself as he made his swing. Actually, those of us who knew this and who watched him closely sometimes saw his lips move. He admitted that he sometimes says it aloud because the act of expressing himself is in accord with his intention to swing almost with reckless abandon. If you find yourself inadvertently holding back when swinging at easy balls, try something similar. Say something explosive, an acceptable expletive perhaps, that induces you to swing forcefully.

"There it is, take it." For another player, a woman who often passed over chances to win points when openings occurred, we coined a more refined expression. However, we often had to rehearse this tactical situation. By my taking a vulnerable position in my court and then feeding easy balls to her she soon learned to recognize that the opportunity to win the point was there: she had only to take it. Try this method. If you feel that you're not making winning shots after having created openings in your opponents' court, practice this way. Have a friend hit softly to you while he or she is deliberately out of position so you can practice your put-aways.

GETTING SET TO HIT: In this sequence the player is shown adjusting her steps as she runs so she can set her left foot down before she makes contact with the ball. Though it doesn't show here, she moved quickly, then slowed down ("fast, then slow") to eliminate as much head and body movement as possible. Nevertheless, here her momentum carried her one step beyond the contact point, as seen in the last frame. Movement is detrimental to vision; whenever possible set a foot down as you swing and as she has done in frame d. ▷

(A)

(B)

(C)

(D)

(E)

(F)

Excellent form on a forehand drive. Note particularly six features: The player is in the ideal, though not always possible or convenient, sideways stance; she is transfering her weight on to her front foot; she has bent her wrist back; she is hitting with a bent arm; she has already turned her hips and shoulders; and she appears to have watched the ball to within a few feet of impact.

"Green means 'go'." When teaching students the proper time during a rally to approach the net, I use the colors of our two-tone red and green court surface. I instruct them to go to the net only when hitting from a location inside their baseline which happens to be the green area of our courts. In a drill I've devised for this purpose. I remind them that the color green signifies "go." They are to go to the net after hitting an aggressive shot from that area of the court. At the same time they learn to remain in the backcourt after hitting a shot from the red area of the court, the area behind the baseline. If you, too, play on two-tone courts like these, this kind of color coding may help you learn when best to go to the net and when to stay in the backcourt. Green signifies "go"; red signifies "stay (back)."

"Touch your thigh," (to provide a reference point for hitters who must learn to lower the racket below the intended point of contact to hit top-spin backhands).

"Position yourself with panicky steps," (to stress careful, calculated moves when getting in position to hit an overhead smash).

"Finish the shot; finish it first." (to change the rhythm of players who prepare for the next stroke too quickly and/or who look up to see the results of a shot before finishing the stroke properly).

"Stroke it smoothly," (to correct a too vigorous swing).

"Spin the serve," (to use on second serves).

"Be light and loose," (to keep from tensing up while in the ready position).

Here I've listed only a few of the cues I've used effectively in my work. You may benefit from them. But you'll probably get more satisfaction from inventing your own cues as you try to put your feelings into words during practice and play. This will require conscious thought on your part. And this, of course, is in keeping with the theme of this book: To play well, think about how to play.

Pam Shriver tells us what she thought about during an upset win over Navratilova. "During the match I got a little tense," she said. "But I just kept telling myself to reach out for the first serve and to hit the volley. I concentrated on just those two things." Another good example that thinking pays off.

SUMMARY. The same cues you used in practice can be used in play to offset tension. By thinking of something positive to do, as suggested by a cue, you can avoid negative thoughts such as the fear of missing. Knowing that you usually make a certain shot in practice will enable you to hit more confidently in play.

Chris Evert Lloyd, one of the best groundstrokers in tennis history, swings with a flatter stroke and hits with less topspin (often none at all) than many poorer strokers. A great deal of topspin, though ensuring that the ball will drop sharply, may make it difficult for you to control the depth of your shots. You may hit with better depth if you hit with less spin. To do so, make your swing plane flatter, more toward the plane in which your racket faces, as Lloyd does.

CHAPTER **7**

USE YOUR MIND
AND YOUR RACKET

OOOOOOOOOOOOOOOOOOOOOOOOOOOOOOOOOO

Shortly before writing this chapter, I had the good fortune to see a tension-filled match between Chris Evert Lloyd and Tracy Austin. The match, played as part of a four-player challenge tournament in La Costa, California, was televised nationally, so you may have seen it too. If so, you'll recall that Lloyd won what was essentially an hour-and-a-half baseline duel.

As is usually the case when these two play each other, there were several long rallies. Some were exceptionally long. The ball once crossed the net sixty-four times, and on a few other occasions, more than fifty.

My oldest son Tom was watching the match with me and he, too, was impressed with the length of the rallies. Being inexperienced in tournament play and admitting that he easily becomes unnerved in matches, he wondered aloud, "Gosh, how can they be so calm? What are they thinking of during those long rallies?"

What he wanted to know, of course, was what *he* should be thinking of during *his* rallies. Chances are you ask that same thing about yourself, about your own game.

Which brings me to the main point of this chapter. Here I'll explain what probably goes on in the minds of tournament players during play. And I'll indicate the right things for you to think about while you play.

ACTIVATE YOUR MIND

Let's start by pretending I'm playing a point against an imaginary opponent. Pretend also that you're moving along closely beside me, close enough to hear my remarks. I'll think aloud so you'll know what I'm thinking. And since I've always been a better-than-average baseline rallier, my thoughts during the rally are as good a model as you're likely to find.

At this hypothetical point, I've just returned my opponent's serve and he and I are starting a rally. Here comes his shot and here's what I say.

· "Ah, he's hitting to my forehand. Only two steps to my right and I'll have an easy, high shot. Looks like I'll have a chance to move him deep on his backhand. No problem there: I've made that shot many times before.

"There it goes, right where I aimed. But that will give him a chance to angle a crosscourt to my backhand, so I'd better hurry back to the center mark.

"Ah! Just as I figured. Here it comes to my backhand, fairly soft, waist high, and easily within reach. Hey, this gives me a chance to put him in trouble. He's kind of deep, so a short angle to his backhand may be hard to handle.

"Son-of-a-gun, he got to it easily and . . . oh, oh, he's done the same thing to me. Now I'll have to scramble for his short shot to *my* backhand.

"No bother now. I'll get there in time. Better be careful, though; it's a low ball, so I'll have to lift it a bit. A slice will do the job. Well, look at that; he's not getting back to the center mark in time. Oh boy, a slice down the line should give him trouble.

"There it goes, low and deep, just as I planned.

"And here comes his return. Ah there it goes, into the net.

"Love, fifteen."

Of course, it isn't as easy to win a point as I make it sound here. I'll not always be able to predict my opponent's shot accurately. Neither will I always be able to place my own shots accurately. But shot making is another matter that I discussed elsewhere in this book. Here we're more concerned with what to think about during play.

When you visualize this monologue and this point being played, assume that I'm in the second of our two levels of development. I'm able to stroke automatically because of many hours, days, weeks, months, and years I've practiced strokes.

The practice has served its purpose. I'm now able to make the strokes while not having to think about them. And so my mind is free to perceive, to take in, the entire situation.

The word "perceive" is important here. It means more than seeing; it implies understanding along with seeing. My eyes and my mind notice several things: my opponent's location; the kind of stroke he's making; the speed, direction, and trajectory of his shot; my distance to run to reach his shot; the height of the bounce as I prepare my stroke; and his location just before I hit.

As I notice what my opponent is doing, what kind of stroke he's making, I must also anticipate or predict the result of his stroke. For example, if he's swinging markedly in a downward plane, I conclude that he's going to put backspin on the ball. I next notice the trajectory of his shot. And I'm able to predict the bounce of his shot. As a result, I'll almost always be prepared for whatever kind of bounce. The bounce as a result of his spin may bother me. But it will never fool me, never take me by surprise. It's simply a matter of applying what I see and what I know. To say it in other words, a matter of using my mind, of being a thinking player.

All this thinking is done quickly, much more quickly than I can say it in words. And if I think of my strokes at all, it's only to decide whether to drive or to slice, to hit flat or with top spin, to hit hard or softly. In other words, I make a kind of general decision; I don't think much about the mechanics of strokes, during play.

If this sounds like a large order, recall that you do something like it every time you drive your car through heavy traffic. You make yourself aware of the environment around you. You notice the green traffic light up ahead that will probably turn red before you get that far. You also see a pedestrian about to enter a cross-walk even closer to you. And there's a car following very closely behind you, too close, you decide. So you slow down gradually. And since there's no on-coming traffic and you're in the proper lane, you decide to turn left into the supermarket lot.

You take all this in quickly. And you make these decisions quickly. But you also shift gears, turn on signal lights, apply brake pressure, and turn the wheel, all without thinking.

You are able to take in all this information and are able to re-spond properly to it because of your experience. But if you recall, when you were first learning to drive you were very uncomfortable in similar situations. There seemed to be too much to notice, too much to think about, too much to react to. And so you probably made a few mistakes, possible scraping a fender or two, but, let's hope, not running down a pedestrian.

Soon however, you were able to react more calmly. You learned to see all the objects and events laid out before you (and the car follow-ing behind you) and you made a decision to act, a decision in which you accommodated to all those objects and events.

I'm suggesting that you and I go through similar experiences on the tennis court. We have to learn to recognize what's going on during a point, both on our side of the net and across the net. In short, we have to perceive the situation so we can direct our attention properly and can react properly.

CONTROL YOUR ATTENTIONAL RANGE

You must be able to widen and to narrow your attention span during play as play situations change. During a doubles match, for example, while moving into position to hit a groundstroke, you may be able to notice the locations of the other three players on the court. You may notice that your partner is one step inside the service line and that one of the opponents is in a similar location on the other side of the net. You may also notice that the other opponent is stroking from the baseline and is running to the net after his or her shot.

Because one opponent is already at the net you wisely decide to hit a low shot to the net-rusher's feet. As you take in this situation and as you make this decision you may also notice that the on-coming ball has a great deal of top-spin. This is not surprising to you because you saw that your opponent had swung markedly upward and that the shot was arched in flight. You then properly predict a high bounce and adjust your swing accordingly. We can say then that you had a broad attentional focus, and that it served you well in this situation. You were able to notice several situational cues and were able to take in a great deal of situational information.

Though your broad focus helped you make the right play in our hypothetical situation, you may best shift to a narrow focus in other tactical situations. Let's say, for example, that you find yourself having to pass a net man in singles. As you move into position for your shot you decide where to hit. With that decision made, you hit as you planned, down-the-line, let's say, with little or no concern for your opponent's location. You focus your attention on the ball so you can judge it and time it accurately. Then when you feel those matters are taken care of you may shift your attention to some suitable cue you've used in practice to make this kind of shot (perhaps a lowered rear shoulder). Here your narrow focus of attention is perfectly suitable and it lets you respond properly to this particular situation.

A third situation, one which you'll handle best by narrowing your attention range even more, occurs when you're returning cannon-ball serves. Here, everything happens too quickly for you to change your intentions or your stroke after the server hits the ball. And so it's useless to have alternate plans and to intend to use one or the other. Instead, you must carry on with your one and original plan.

You've probably learned from experience that your best play here is to merely block the ball rather than to swing at it with a lengthy stroke. But you may not be aware of your best choice of shots. I suggest, therefore, that you use the kind of shot you have most confidence in (either slice, flat, or top-spin) and that you hit in the direction you are most often successful with. In other words, if you hit crosscourt better than down the line, hit crosscourt a large majority of the time. And if you have better control of your slice, use that stroke rather than a more spectacular, but undependable, top-spin drive. All of this implies, of course, that you've become aware of your strengths and weaknesses, of your preferences and dislikes, through experience in practice and in play. Which, I'm sure you'll agree, reinforces my contention that thinking about how you play is the best way to learn to play better.

To learn how to get into a suitable frame of mind for the difficult task of returning hard serves, consider what Ted Williams, baseball's great batter, says of a similar situation. Batting, Williams says, is a personal duel, a test of skill and will, between the pitcher and the batter. He goes on to say that he blocks out all distracting influences as he faces the pitcher and that he thinks only of doing his best in this one-on-one situation. This may be a good plan for you too. Momentarily, forget about the score, about the crucialness of the situation, about the consequences of losing. Instead, concentrate only on winning that one point, that personal duel between you and the server. Play each point one at a time. Accept each challenge one at a time. In each situation, plan to do what you believe you do best. Then go ahead with your plan.

I've helped many students feel more positive about their ability to handle fast serves by using this metaphor with them. If it didn't make them more confident, at the very least it made them less fearful.

FOCUS ON THE ACTION

You may learn to control your attention span during play by pretending your brain functions like a camera.

During competition while your opponent is hitting the ball, "take a picture" of the total scene, a panoramic view, as it were. Notice your opponent's location and his or her swing. Be aware of your location. For all of this, imagine that you have a wide-angle lens in your mind's camera.

But once your opponent hits and you're moving into position to return the ball, you'll want to see it clearly in order to judge accurately its trajectory, speed, and direction. And as the ball gets progressively closer to you, you'll want to focus on it to make a solid hit. For this, imagine you've changed to a close-up lens. Then take an imaginary close-up picture of the ball.

Meanwhile, you'll want to remain aware of your opponent's location while also being aware of yours. Carry these impressions in your mind as a kind of after-image to help you choose your shot properly.

As you prepare to make your stroke and while making it, with your mind's camera take another picture. Visualize the shot you want to make. See it in your mind's eye as you swing.

One way to do this is to imagine that the ball, as it leaves your racket, is trailing a streamer of smoke behind it. Imagine that you can see the smoke rising from your contact point, clearing the net, and landing at your intended aim point.

When you're preparing to serve you have time to reverse this image. In your mind's eye, "see" the ball returning to you. Imagine that it's rising from its aim point and moving backward through space, along the same flight path and in the same trajectory you "saw" it move forward earlier. In your imagination, move the ball back and forth that way. I know this kind of imagery works for many of my students. It's likely to work for you too.

DEVISE A GAME PLAN

A thinking player thinks before the match, during the match, and after the match. A good part of your before-the-match-thinking should be spent on devising a game plan. You've probably heard of football games that were supposedly won or lost in the locker room at the chalkboard. This is another way of saying a team planned properly or improperly how they were going to play that game.

Make a game plan in tennis for the same reason. Decide what your opponent can't do well. Then decide how your strength matches up with your opponent's weakness.

Consider the opposite, too. Where is your opponent strong? How well can you defend yourself against that strength? On the basis of this decision, plan your strategy and tactics.

To plan properly, distinguish between the meanings of those two terms. "Strategy" refers to a broad plan. For example, you may decide that your chances for winning are best if you rush to the net so you can use your strong volleys. But you must first decide what tactics will best enable you to do that.

Should you run up behind your serve? Or should you rally first and then go up behind a groundstroke? Where should you place your groundstroke, to your opponent's backhand or forehand? And what kind of shot should you make on your approach shot, a slice or a drive, deep or very short?

Perhaps one of the best-known examples of an effective game plan occurred in the men's final match at Wimbleton in 1976.

Millions of TV viewers saw Arthur Ashe play completely differently from his usual style to upset favored Jimmy Connors. Ashe served slices wide to Connor's two-handed shot, normally a lethal weapon. But Ashe reasoned properly that Connors couldn't do much with that stroke when hitting from wide of the sidelines. As a result, Ashe scored many point-winning volleys off Connors' return of serve.

On alternate games when Connors served, Ashe softened his groundstrokes to make Connors apply all the pace to his own shots. And even more surprisingly, Ashe sliced balls low and short to Connors' forehand, reasoning that Jimmy wouldn't be able to hit those shots aggressively. Jimmy refused to temper his shots against those tactics and made many errors. Those errors, together with his ineffective service returns, led to his defeat.

It may surprise you to learn that Ashe said he was lucky. He explained that on that particular June day the sky was overcast, which was to his advantage. Had it been sunny, he wouldn't have been able to toss the ball to the proper location for his slice serve because the glare of the sun in the background would have made it difficult to see the ball. He's never explained what he'd have done if it had been a bright, sunny day. Nevertheless, we should remember his example of how thinking helps win tennis matches.

WARM-UP

Your on-the-court thinking begins with the pre-match warm-up. So now let's pretend we're concerned with serious tournament play rather than friendly, social play.

Normally tournament committees limit the amount of practice time allotted to competitors. And usually it's too little time for anyone to warm-up properly.

The solution to this is to warm-up elsewhere if possible. Do it as close to your scheduled starting time as possible, but even hours before if necessary. It may surprise you to know that world-class players often warm-up for as long as an hour, off on side courts somewhere, before their matches. They usually shower, change clothes, and freshen up a bit before moving on to the tournament court.

But many players, Guillermo Vilas for one, prefer to go directly from a practice court to the match court. He uses the practice-court time to tune up mentally, to psyche himself up, as well as to loosen up physically for his match. This may be an effective way for you to prepare, too.

During the warm-up period, try to find out what part of your game is working best for you. Find out what isn't working, too. Accept the fact that a cue that helps you hit well one day may not work the next day. And a feeling you have on a particular stroke one day may not be there the next (recall Tom Watson's remarks on this).

Professional golfers know this. That's why they spend so much time on the practice tee immediately before beginning play. One golfer explained it by saying he's trying to find his tendency of the day. Is he fading or hooking? Hitting too low or too high? And while he's still

Use the pre-match, warm-up period to get familiar with the speed, spin, trajectory, and bounce of your opponent's shots. Here, the player has moved back from her baseline to let the ball ascend to chest height, where it leveled off and permitted her to hit "straight away," parallel to the ground. As a result, she had fewer variables to consider as she planned the setting of her racket.

on the practice tee, he tries to allow for the tendency rather than to correct it in play. Obviously, all of this requires conscious thought.

This happens in tennis, too. Even Pancho Gonzales, one of the best servers of all time, has days when his cannonball serve isn't working. On those days he changes his serving tactics and relies on spin and placement rather than on speed.

Experiment in your pre-match warm-up. For example, if you don't have the touch and sensitivity to slice effectively, don't attempt to slice in your match. If you feel especially quick at the net, plan strategy that gets you to the net. If your groundstrokes feel especially sound, plan to play from the backcourt.

But, of course, the more you have working for you, the better your chances of winning. So use the warm-up to try to get things working. To emphasize that point I like to refer to that procedure as "tuning up," which implies more precision in movement, more attention to detail, than does "warming up."

TUNE UP TOO

Warming up is generally considered a physical activity during which the player moves about rather slowly (often too slowly, in my opinion) and only gradually speeds up. Many players liken this to the automotive warming up procedure in which the driver waits for the temperature of his engine oil to rise before he revs his engine fast. But as I've suggested earlier, this kind of warming up should be done on a side court before the scheduled match time. Now, on the tournament court, time should be spent more wisely on fine-tuning physical mechanisms (your strokes) and on developing the proper mental set for play. Think of it as tuning up, or perhaps even tuning *in*.

Begin now to focus your attention on the tasks at hand. Specifically, you should now want to regain the feel of your strokes, to gain the sensitivity you are capable of for setting your racket face properly, to notice what your opponent is capable of doing against your shots, and lastly, to get familiar with the speed, spin, and trajectory of your opponent's shots. For this latter purpose, perhaps the most important of all, focus on the ball.

As I've said several times earlier, you'll not have time to do much thinking during a swing. Instead, direct the major part of your conscious energies to the ball so you become familiar with its flight characteristics as they are influenced by your opponent's shots. To say it as I've said it earlier: narrow your attention for a good part of your warm-up period. Logically, this should be the last part of that period (after you've limbered up) because only then will you be facing your opponent's realistic shots, i.e. those made after he or she has limbered up.

This matter of focusing your attention on the ball (in practice, in the warm-up, and in play) requires a great deal of self-discipline. But it pays dividends for two reasons: it keeps you from looking up prematurely (before you've made contact) as many players do who are anxious—too anxious—to see the result of their shot. Secondly, it gets your mind off your opponent and puts it where it should be, for the moment at least, on the ball. Most of us who teach professionally agree that failure to watch the ball, and failure to adjust the swing to it, are the most common faults among our students. Conscious attention to focusing on—or even "tuning in" on—the ball helps most learners overcome these faults.

But here I must warn you of a common misconception about watching the ball, a misconception resulting from erroneous information given to students even by experienced tennis teachers. I'm referring to the suggestion that you see the ball on your racket. It is impossible to do so.

As long as forty years ago many strong, authoritative opinions were expressed against the likelihood of any player seeing the ball on his or her racket. In a survey conducted by American Lawn Tennis magazine (now World Tennis), the leading American players of that time were asked for their opinions on the matter. The players were almost unanimous in saying they could not see the ball on their rackets. But the word "try" was used in over ninety percent of the replies. I have no doubt that if a similar survey were made among today's leading players the replies would be similar: players try to see the ball on their strings but they admit that they cannot.

Nowadays, in athletic research we have the advantage of sophisticated equipment. As a result we have learned that contact occurs for only milliseconds (.0038-.005), far too quickly for the human eye to see. But just as it did forty years ago, it will help you to try to see the ball on your strings. It will help you not only to judge the ball's flight properly and to time your swing accurately, but as is the point of this chapter, to occupy your mind.

THINK BETWEEN POINTS

But now let's consider what you should be thinking of between points. As you walk to retrieve a ball or to change sides try to remember, to recall, what's happened up to this stage in the match. What shots are winning for you? And what tactics? Or, if you're behind the score, what are your opponent's strong shots? And what tactics is he or she using effectively? Where are your errors—and your opponent's—occurring?

In a sense, you should be thinking like a card player who tries to remember what cards were played, who discarded what, who's probably holding what, so he can properly plan his next move.

If you're losing, you'll try to change your shots, of course. If you're winning, you'll plan to continue to play that way, meanwhile being watchful for a change in tactics by your opponent.

Here, again, as I've said before, your mind should be so occupied with such facts that you don't have time to project your thoughts inward and criticize or berate yourself. The next point is far too important to play it while in a detached state of mind. Keep your mind on the important things, the most important of which is either the present point or the ensuing one.

I can remember losing more than one match when I was young and foolish by misdirecting my thoughts when I was behind. I can remember worrying about the effects of losing—how it would hurt my ranking, how it would look in the paper, what my friends would say. But as I grew older and more experienced I learned to blot out such destructive thoughts even when near defeat. I learned to play one point at a time, keeping my mind fully on the tactics and strategy of the match. As a result, I've since saved many more matches this way than I had lost years ago because of losing my concentration. Try this approach; it may work for you too. Take one step at a time, play one point at a time.

I learned a useful metaphor that applies here from one of my students to whom I was expressing these ideas after he and I pulled out a close doubles match from almost certain defeat. "Ah ha," he said, "As Confucious say, 'even the longest journey begins with but a single step'." Confucious may or may not have said it; no matter. But I remember that expression now whenever I fall far behind in the score and have to play catch-up tennis. It helps keep my mind where it belongs: on the facts of the match, the present, not the past or the future. Which is what you should do on every point.

OCCUPY YOUR MIND WITH FACTS

Here are some kinds of things you should be thinking about to occupy your mind. If you're playing a net-rushing game and are losing, evaluate your approach shots, your volleys and your opponent's shots. Are you being passed by very good shots from your opponent or are your approach shots so weak that your opponent gets easy passing shots to make? Or are you not being passed at all but simply missing more volleys than you normally do? This is more likely to occur than is the first condition. Only at top-level play do we see numerous sensational passing shots. At lower levels the losing volleyer misses more often than he/she is passed. If you find yourself in this losing situation the solution is simple enough, in theory; hit better, more aggressive approach shots so you'll have easier volleys to make.

Now let's consider an opposite situation: Your opponent is frequently at the net and those tactics are winning for him or her. Here you must consider, "Is he or she really volleying that well or am I missing so many of my attempts to pass?" Again, I say, the latter is likely to be the case. Time and time again I've tabulated the results of these kinds of shots at all levels of play. My figures convince me that except in top-level play, when a baseliner loses against a net rusher, it's usually because of missed passing shots by the baseliner, rather than because of winning volleys by the opponent. If during a match you conclude that this is true of your game, that you're losing to a net rusher, play your attempts to pass more carefully. Don't hit so close to the lines or to the net. Give yourself a bigger margin of safety. Make your opponent show that he or she can volley well enough to beat you. Don't beat yourself.

Now let's pretend that both you and your opponent are playing mainly from the backcourt, and that you get involved in several long rallies. There's a certain kind of tennis attitude, a tennis mentality, required for this kind of play. Strangely enough, not all players of even world-class ability have it. I'm referring to patience, patience to keep the ball in play while waiting for errors from your opponent or for weak shots that you can hit aggressively to draw errors. For a good example of the negative effects of impatience, consider what Martina Navratilova said after losing badly to Tracy Austin. "I wasn't patient enough after the long rallies," she explained. "I did okay on some rallies but on the next points I didn't want to go through another long rally again so I got impatient and went for winners. That hurt me." All to the delight of young Tracy, I'm sure, who revels in long rallies.

Tracy reveals her contrasting attitude in similar situations with these remarks made after she beat Andrea Jaeger in the U.S. Open. She admitted that the spectators may have been bored with the long backcourt rallies. "But," she added, "I had to be patient. I had to play her game until I got an opening." Another clear lesson, I'm sure you'll agree.

Despite all the physical practice and mental training you do, you'll miss a goodly number of shots. That's inevitable. So let's get back to considering what you should be thinking about between points. Part of your between-the-points thinking should be directed toward the tactics and strategy of the match. But after a missed shot, a good part of it should be on your stroke. Specifically, you should analyze the reason for missing the shot. This gets us back to the fundamental fact of the game: The ball goes mainly where your racket faces. And it also brings us back to the main theme of this book, the anti-inner game theme. Think about how to play while you're playing.

To be specific here, let's consider that you hit a forehand drive into the net. As you walk to retrieve the ball consider why you missed.

Unless you hit too softly (which isn't likely unless you tried a drop shot), you probably had your racket face closed slightly at impact. So try to recall the feel of that missed shot. Replay the stroke in your mind and visualize the improper position of your elbow, forearm, wrist, or hand, whichever it was that caused you to set your racket inaccurately. Immediately visualize the proper position of that joint or that body segment. Then plan to make a correction the next time you get a similar shot to play. It may help if you make a swing at an imaginary ball, doing it as you know you should have done it.

You may recall seeing even very good players do this. It may appear that they are berating themselves for stupid action but it's more likely that they are trying to dispel the feeling of that improper stroke that caused the missed shot. John McEnroe, however, uses this kind of pantomime in reverse. When he makes what he considers a foolish, easy miss he often swings at an imaginary ball while making that same physical error in his stroke. Several times I've seen him hit an imaginary forehand while raising his elbow as his racket passes through the hitting area. This action causes his racket to face downward at impact, causing the ball to go into the net. He exaggerates the wrong elbow position seemingly to signify that he knows why he missed it. "So let's do it differently (and better) next time, you lunk head," he seems to be saying to himself.

SUMMARY. During play, be attentive to what's going on in your match. If things are not going to your advantage try to figure out what to do about it. If you're losing, try to change your shots and/or your tactics. If you've won a majority of the recent points, try to duplicate those conditions. Your mind should be so occupied with such thoughts that you don't have time to get mad over your errors, or to be distracted by crowd noises or by balls or players on adjacent courts. Neither do you have time to worry about the consequences of missing the next shot or of losing the game and/or the match.

CHAPTER 8

LEARN HOW TO CONTROL TENSION

OOOOOOOOOOOOOOOOOOOOOOOOOOOOOOOOOOOOOOO

During my many years as Head Professional at the Broadmoor Hotel in Colorado Springs we've had several big-name players conduct clinics and exhibitions for our club members and hotel guests. The best known of these players was Jack Kramer, former Wimbledon, U.S., and World Professional Champion. Our instructional sessions at those clinics always concluded with question-and-answer sessions in which the guest pro replied to queries of the participants. During one of Kramers's clinics he was asked how he managed to avoid the nervousness that regularly develops from the pressure of match play. He smiled at that question, then related how he and Tom Brown, playing each other in a Wimbledon final, had trouble even warming up.

Dramatizing it for the crowd's amusement, he explained, "I'd bounce the ball and hit it into the net. Tom would bounce it and hit into the back fence. I'd try again and hit too long. Tom would try again and hit into the net. There we were," he continued, "supposedly the two best players in the world, and we were so nervous we couldn't even get a rally started in the warm-up. And you're asking me how to deal with pressure."

After the laughter subsided, however, Jack went on to explain that once play had begun, both he and Tom got so involved in the technicalities of play, of the strategies and tactics of it, that the feeling of pressure gradually subsided until it disappeared almost completely. It did at least for him and he gradually gained the upper hand and won.

But Kramer had confidence in his strokes because he knew, through endless hours of practice, that he could produce winning shots with them. Not being fearful that his strokes would fail him, that he would miss shots that he normally made, he relaxed mentally and was able to play his normal game. And since he was the best shot maker in the world, he won handily despite his early nervousness.

I could see at that clinic that Kramer's answer didn't satisfy the man who asked the question. Though Kramer explained that he was too busy with the facts of the match to worry about the outcome of it, or about the result of one particular stroke or shot, he didn't explain how we can concentrate so much on the match that we become oblivious to the many pressure-inducing events connected with it. He explained what happened but he didn't explain how to make it happen. This chapter is written to correct that oversight, to augment Kramer's explanation. Now, since we are going to discuss pressure, we must first define the term.

STRESS AND PRESSURE DEFINED

Though psychologists usually use more learned terms to describe it (to them, pressure is a perceived threat to a person's survival, welfare, self-worth or esteem), in tennis we can say simply that it is the fear of losing, or of missing a shot, or even of looking bad while winning. If you recall tense moments of your important matches, you'll agree that you feared one or another of these consequences.

Lest you think these kinds of match jitters are unusual, let me point out that Chris Evert Lloyd said she became ill from tension immediately before her first match against young Tracy Austin. It's not unusual for athletes to feel this way before a pressure contest. Though the effects of anxiety (in Chris's case here, the fear of losing) vary among individuals, nausea, light-headedness, perceived weakness, and trembling are fairly common symptoms of it. Obviously, even with her outstanding record as a player, Chris is only human.

The same can be said for Tracy, who had this to say when reporters asked if she was nervous before her first match against (then) teen-age sensation Andrea Jaeger: " . . . it [pressure] makes me play better. The more nervous I am the better I play." Though the latter part of her statement may not be true, for reasons I'll explain later, we see that by her own admission, she feels the same effects of pressure the rest of us do.

More recently, Martina Navratilova explained after a match that she expected to play well because before the match she was "nervous, just the right amount. But after we got started, I relaxed and began to play real loose." And again from golf, Tom Watson tells us he was so nervous he almost jumped out of his skin during the final round of the 1980 Masters tourney, which he won over Jack Nicklaus. Surely when players of their stature admit they feel pressure during play, the rest of us should feel it too. But the problem remains, how do we deal with pressure, or tension, or stress or whatever you want to call it, for the terms can be used synonomously.

The first step in dealing with it is to recognize its symptoms. Stress is a hyper-emotional state and is revealed by increased muscular tension, especially in the shoulders and neck. With that increased tension, some of the muscles in those regions don't always relax as they should to permit complete freedom of movement around the joints they control. As a result, they often interfere with other muscles that are the primary movers around those joints. Consequently, many players do actually feel tight at those critical joint movements, hence the description "tightening up." And as they tighten up, their timing and coordination deteriorates.

There are several other common physical symptoms of the stress one feels in competition. Physically, it quickens your pulse rate, raises your blood pressure, interferes with digestion, and results in a general feeling of unpleasantness. Most of these symptoms are measurable so we know they occur.

One of the most frequently mentioned symptoms of pressure and tension is referred to as "choking." If match tension is severe enough, it may affect your timing, your judgment, and your coordination. If you play badly as a result, we can say you choked. It happens to even the best players. Tracy Austin, for example, willingly admitted that she choked while playing a tie-breaker against Kerry Reid. And John McEnroe occasionally makes the choke gesture (he places one hand on his throat and encircles it with the thumb and forefinger) to signify that he missed that particular shot for that reason.

Like Austin and McEnroe, you, too, are likely to feel mental tension and the physical symptom of choking in any match that is important to you. When you want badly to win or at least to play well you'll probably begin to feel slightly uncomfortable—nervous, fidgety, and edgy. You may deal better with this phenomenon of choking if you understand it.

The word is applied universally in tennis and in other sports because of physiological responses that occur when playing in pressure situations. Saliva glands and mucus-secreting glands are inhibited and some tension develops in the throat muscles. The combined effects of these responses is to make swallowing difficult. Hence the word "choking" to describe this condition.

After recognizing the symptoms, we must consider that there is good and bad pressure. Good pressure is part of being "up" for a match, a kind of heightened sensitivity and increased energy. In high school psychology class you called that state of mind the fight-or-flight syndrome that often enables humans to perform beyond their normal capabilities.

In sports this same mental state and the physical effects it causes sometimes let us play better than we think we are capable of. Or at least it helps us play closer to our potential. For example, consider there remarks made by U.S. Olympic skater Beth Heiden after she skated a poor race. "I wish I'd been a little more nervous. I was almost too relaxed to do as well as I'd hoped." She's implying, of course, that she had to do without the facilitating effect of nervousness and as a result didn't do too well.

CONTROL YOUR AROUSAL LEVEL

At frequent intervals before and during a match, take note of your mental state, of the amount of pressure you feel. And understand what it's doing to you. In a pressure situation you'll almost certainly feel some anxiety for reasons I've already described (fear of losing or of missing). That anxiety will lead to changes in your attention level, in your emotional state, and in the degree of sensitivity in your joint

Though many good strokers start their forward swings with their racket faces closed, the author uses a different method for this waist-high rising ball. To shape his backswing his swing thought has always been—and could have been here—"keep the racket face vertical, as if standing on edge." Planning such positive action is one good way to avoid negative thoughts, such as the fear of missing.

receptors. And as these change, so does the degree to which you are ready to play to your potential change. This state, this condition in which you find yourself as a result of match pressure, is referred to by sports psychologists as your level of arousal. They tell us that each of us has his or her own best level of arousal, of alertness and excitability, for maximum performance. And the level varies among us as our skill levels vary.

Empirical evidence seems to indicate that there is probably an optimum level of arousal, a small range perhaps, within which a player is likely to perform best. A player not excited to that level is not likely to give a maximum performance. One excited beyond it plays badly, too.

As a beginner your performance during practice or play was probably disrupted when you were excited. Most low-level learners perform badly under pressure, under stress. But as your skill level rose, so did your ability to handle excitement and anxiety. To put it another way, the higher your skill level, the higher your arousal can be without disrupting your performance. In fact, you may even begin to recognize the beneficial effect that Beth Heiden missed.

Simply by accepting nervousness as one of the conditions of play, you may begin to benefit from it. Instead of regarding it as an enemy, a nuisance, a deterrent that you wish would simply go away, be glad you're nervous, knowing that it's making you ready for good performance. That's what nature is doing for you, making you more alert, quicker, more responsive, and even stronger physically. Provided, of course, your nervousness doesn't increase to the point of causing so much muscle tension that you're unable to make the finely coordinated moves you're generally capable of.

For proof that nervousness can help, consider what happens in competitive swimming and track. In those sports accurate, objective measurement of the results of performance is regularly made during both practice and competition. World records are seldom broken in practice. But we see new records set time and time again in competition, when those athletes are keyed up for big events. Plainly, the pressure helps them perform better.

But we also notice that a high state of arousal or excitement may be advantageous in one activity (boxing or football, for example) and yet be detrimental in another activity (bowling, golf putting). To state if differently, we can say that the optimum level of arousal varies from sport to sport. It also varies from person to person. Furthermore, for even the same person, the optimum level may vary from day to day.

And so no one can say dogmatically that you should get aroused to such and such a degree in order to play your best. Instead, we can only generalize on the basis of the results of numerous studies made on athletes in several sports. From those we can conclude that arousal to a level somewhere between excitement and indifference, and slightly closer to the latter, is likely to lead to best performance in tennis.

But still the problem remains: **How** can you regulate your excitement and learn to use it to your advantage?

This is not easy to answer because, as I've said earlier, the effects of arousal vary from person to person. And so do the effectiveness of various de-arousal techniques vary from person to person.

CONTROL PRE-MATCH TENSION

There are several things you can do before a match to reduce arousal during it. Of those I list here, some appear to be contradictory but I've seen each of them work for one player or another. Experiment with them, they may have a similar beneficial effect on you.

Try to find a quiet, comfortable site where you can be alone with your thoughts. Try to think of happy things that quiet your mind. A day at the beach or in the mountains or on a ski slope or a fishing stream—whatever you remember as a pleasant, happy experience can help you relax for play if you train yourself to reminisce momentarily before facing stressful situations.

Try isolating yourself so you can think about and can plan your match strategy. Play the match in your imagination. But see yourself winning. Visualize the shots you feel you are capable of making and pretend they are winning for you. Visualize your opponent's attempts to return your shots. And see yourself intercepting the return shots and making winners from them.

But you may reduce a pressure by preparing in an opposite way. Get your mind completely off the match, however you can best manage to do so. For example, Masters' golf champion Tom Watson studies auto mechanics books. He says he begins to psyche up for the match only when he begins to dress for it in the locker room.

If you feel you need to reduce your anxiety, do things that have a soothing effect on you. Perhaps read, as Watson does. Or listen to your favorite music. For example, a good friend of mine admits that hearing the late Bing Crosby sing "Sweet Leilani" has a soothing effect on him. He's learned to use that as an anti-tension device, humming the song aloud as he dresses for play and during warm-up. He's convinced it often keeps him from tensing up; it relaxes him and lets him play more to his potential.

And still different methods may work better. Mix socially with a group of friends who are not interested in your match. With your mind on other things, you're not likely to develop the muscular tension that accompanies mental tension. You're likely to play better as a result.

Further, I suggest that a moderate amount of physical exercise taken slightly before competition can loosen you up physically and relax you mentally. A few minutes of your typical stretching exercises, some "jumping jacks," burpees, sit-ups, and half-knee bends, followed by some easy jogging or running in place can all help. That may be all you need to ease physical and mental tension as you prepare for a match.

In addition to what I've suggested above, there are other more practical devices you can use to control arousal or to at least reduce it. If you're new in the game, or in the event, or in the environment, you'll probably feel more stress than will another person who is on more familiar ground. The solution to this is to become familiar with the scene, the tournament, the courts, the club house, other competitors, and especially the kind of player you will have to compete against.

I believe so strongly in this that I often advise young coaches to take their young proteges to tournament sites as early as possible before the starting date of the tournament. Time and time again I've seen better players lose because they've played under what they called "strange conditions." Even when I tried to explain humorously that the court was the same dimensions, the net the same height, and the balls and racket identical to what they've used often before, these players still maintained that conditions were different. One particularly bright player said he couldn't "identify with the reality of the situation."

Regardless of whether you can practice at the stressful site, practice under game-like conditions. If your match is to be scored in pro sets, or by tie-breaking procedures, play practice matches in which you score that way. And if you're to play at a windy site, or in a glaring sun, find those kinds of conditions in which to practice. And certainly you should practice on the same kind of surface your match is to be played on. All this is part of being familiar with the scene, of becoming comfortable in the tournament environment. All of this can help reduce pre-match jitters and can help put you in the confident frame of mind that lets you play up to your capabilities.

Look, Act, And Think Like A Winner

One way to approach a match with confidence is to make yourself ready to play. This begins, naturally, with your dress. Your appearance, or at least your impression of what you appear to be, can affect how you feel. To feel like a player, dress like a player: You're more likely to feel ready to do your best if you know you've dressed your best, neatly, comfortably, and appropriately.

I had this impressed upon me rather forcefully one season while I was coaching high school tennis. Two boys on my team, both exper-

Difficult recovery shots such as this are often reflexive, done without conscious thought, as if the player were in the so-called "zone." But it is practice at making a variety of moves in a variety of postures and positions that enables a player to adapt to such unusual situations. Regarding the zone, Pam Shriver says that if there is one, it is simply a condition in which the things a player has been taught and has practiced seem easier to do. Players of her caliber especially appreciate the value of practice and of thinking during practice.

ienced tournament players, requested that they be permitted to wear their own conventional white tennis clothes for team matches rather than to wear our school's maroon and gold uniforms. The players explained that they just didn't feel ready to play a serious tennis match dressed as basketball players. That statement alone induced me to grant their request. They were relieved, and told me several times later how much more confident they felt dressed as tournament players. You, too, are more likely to feel like a winner when you dress like one. Knowing that you fit into the tournament scene, at least in outward appearance, is in itself a confidence builder.

One way to reduce mental tension as you prepare for a match is to maintain a positive, happy attitude—or at least by pretending to be that way. As you arrive at the tournament site, make yourself like what you see. Trick yourself into feeling that way. If it's a crowded noisy scene, tell yourself it's pleasantly exciting. If there's a schedule delay and you have to wait beyond your assigned starting time, don't let that disturb you. Accept it as part of the game. You may be more inclined to do so if I remind you that at world-class tournaments (such as the U.S. Open), matches are not scheduled to start at specific times. Instead, players are told that they will play the second, third, fourth, or whatever numbered match on a particular court and they have to be ready whenever the preceding match ends.

As you take the court to begin your warm-up, let your opponent know how pleased you are with the setting and with the opportunity to play him or her under the existing conditions, whatever they are. If it's windy, say how much you like playing in a refreshing breeze. If it's hot and humid, say how loose and limber such weather makes you feel. If it's cool and cloudy, say how invigorating it is. Look around at the court scene, show that it all pleases you. God is in the heavens and the world is spinning happily. Oh, what a great day for a match! Tell yourself so. And let your opponent see that you feel that way.

After surveying the scene and showing how pleased you are, become a "take charge" person. Act like an experienced tournament player and pretend this is all old stuff to you. Spin the racket for side or serve. Measure the net. Test your string tension and show that you're satisfied with it. Stretch a bit, and jog in place. Stoop, squat, and bend to limber up. Show how fit you are. Show that you're all tuned up and eager to get started. You can often gain a psychological edge this way even before play begins.

Determine Your Best Mental State

Despite these attempts to prepare psychologically for your match, once play begins you're likely to be involved in any number of anxiety-inducing situations. How you may best cope with them is the subject of the remainder of this chapter. I feel that this material may be the meatiest part of this book, especially since my intention through-out has been to help you integrate such mental aspects of play with the physical aspects discussed earlier.

I've already suggested that there is probably a personal best level of arousal as you prepare for a match and as you play it. The question arising now is how to get into that optimum level. Specifically, should you psyche yourself up or calm yourself down.

To determine the best course of action, try to recall how you felt when you last played especially well. Chances are you were a little higher than totally relaxed and quite a lot lower than very nervous. Recall that Beth Heiden said she was too relaxed and that Tracy Austin says she plays better when she's nervous. Some reminiscing of your better matches should help you recognize your best mental state. To put yourself there it may help if we discuss how you can control mental tension.

Physiological reaction to stress and anxiety can be controlled in several ways. Among them are various relaxation techniques, includ-ing hypnosis and Transcendental Meditation, to control muscle ten-sion and to minimize tension levels.

In tennis, TM is mentioned more frequently partly because millions of TV viewers believe they saw Arthur Ashe meditating during a side change-over in his Wimbledon final match against Connors. But the fact is that Ashe had not gotten into TM until several months after that match. When asked what he was thinking of as he sat there with his head down and eyes closed, he replied that he was planning his strategy, some of which was described here in an earlier chapter.

If you are inclined to meditate to improve your tennis, consider this. Although there is evidence to show that meditators are able to control some body responses that are linked to anxiety, at least two studies made in motor learning laboratories suggest that the value of Transcendental Meditation for improving physical performance by reducing arousal levels must be questioned.

The results of these studies show that the effects of meditation might well be detrimental. At least they were in these simple labora-tory tests of pursuit rotor tracking ability. The researchers suggest that the state of deep relaxation induced by meditation seemed to have too strong a de-arousal effect, and as a result, the subjects being tested didn't perform well. This disputes the inner games thesis that you'll play better when completely relaxed.

PSYCHE YOURSELF UP

If you've watched either Jimmy Connors or Billie Jean King play, surely you've seen them appear to berate themselves after making an error and to congratulate themselves after making a good shot. It's easy to see that neither of them is as relaxed as inner game suggests you should be. Rather, King and Connors appear to be psyching themselves up, raising their levels of arousal for the ensuing points.

As regards this matter of temperament during play, Connors says he hates the ball. The vigor and effort with which he swings and the facial expressions he makes seem to confirm that he's far from relaxed when he plays. And, among the women players, Pam Shriver's coach urges her to continue to "punish the ball," a trait he noticed in her when he first saw her play in her pre-teen years. He believes she plays better when she's in that frame of mind, not when she's relaxed and playing casually.

From Connors' and Shriver's aggressive attitudes we may conclude that if you don't care about winning or losing, play *with* the ball. Chances are you'll also be playing *with* your opponent rather than against him or her. And if to you the game is mainly an art form, you may prefer to apply such a soft, benevolent approach to the matter of stroking the ball.

But if you consider the game an athletic contest to be won or lost according to the relative abilities of the opposing players, you had better start doing things to the ball that are to your advantage. In other words, go at it agressively as Jimmy Connors and Pam Shriver are known to do.

For one last example of a winning competitive temperament let me tell you about Ingemar Stenmark, Sweden's Olympic ski champion. He says he reduces pre-race nervousness by making himself angry, at himself, the race officials, the crowd—anyone. He explains that the gestures he then makes, a clenched fist, a slap on the thigh, have a physiological effect on his legs and as a result, he stops feeling shaky and he feels in better control of them.

CALM YOURSELF DOWN

Despite these examples of aggressive winning temperament, I've learned from my students that most of them have the reverse problem. Instead of psyching themselves up as do Connors, King, Jaeger, and Stenmark, they need to calm themselves down, to reduce arousal from the level engendered by a pressure situation. For purposes of this discussion of dealing with pressure, I'm assuming you're a typical student with a typical need—to reduce tension. I'm also assuming that you're not likely to be so committed to the game that you will undergo hypnosis or become a meditator. If I've judged you correctly, you may benefit from devising your own relaxation techniques.

As I've said earlier, one effect of mental pressure is muscle tension. Staying cool under that pressure is a matter of reducing that tension. But you don't need costly, esoteric methods to do so. You can probably learn to handle it with some simple exercises that can be done both off and on the court.

One method is to simply practice contracting and relaxing muscles at will. This is easy enough to do because much muscular contraction is under direct voluntary control. Prove this to yourself. Let your right arm hang limp at your side and place your left hand on your triceps muscle, the one on the back and the outside of your arm, close to your shoulder. As your arm hangs loosely (due to gravity pulling it down), you'll feel that your triceps muscle is relaxed, soft. Now straighten your arm as much as possible trying to stretch your fingers to the ground. As you do that, you'll feel the muscle tighten because that's its chief function: to extend your arm at the elbow. Speaking technically, we can say it is the prime mover for arm extension.

Meanwhile, another prominent muscle in your arm, the biceps (in front, between the elbow and shoulder), is completely relaxed. Move your left hand to it and you'll feel that it's soft as it must be to allow full extension of your arm. If it were contracted instead, it would inhibit full arm extension and so technically we could say it is antagonistic to the movement.

Now if you bend your arm at the elbow, you'll feel the biceps contracting while the triceps relaxes. Here the biceps is the prime mover and the triceps is the antagonist. This kind of reciprocal action goes on constantly during physical activity. This is not to say one set of muscles relaxes completely while the other contracts fully. Instead, the antagonists must often be in a state of partial contraction to provide a steadying, stabilizing influence on the bony structures involved. Meanwhile, the prime movers may also be only partially contracted if only a partial contraction is sufficient for the task at hand. Skill in swinging your racket depends in large measure on how accurately you control the amount of contraction and/or relaxation in the muscles involved.

With this explanation, you may understand why "tightening up" when playing under pressure is an apt description of what goes on during a swing. The antagonist muscles don't relax sufficiently. As a result, they interfere with the movement intended by the prime movers and often the stroke is not as smooth nor as fluent as the player is able to make under more relaxed conditions.

You have the same kind of voluntary control over most muscles involved in a tennis stroke. The ones to be mainly concerned with are those of the shoulder, neck and arm (the levator scapulae, the trapezius and the rotator cuff). Just as you did when bending and straightening your arm, make several imaginary tennis swings while being attentive to the different degrees of tension you can develop. Experiment while hitting balls in practice, too. Notice especially the effect of the various tension levels on your shots. You'll probably find that high tension is detrimental to your shots and that a tension level somewhere between high and low, and probably closer to the latter, gives best results.

This kind of practice should make you aware of muscle tension when it develops during a match. Recognizing tension is the first step in dealing with it. And since in this practice you learned that you can reduce muscle tension at will, you should be able to do so in competition.

CONTROL YOUR BREATHING

One way to get the relaxed muscle states you want is to control your breathing. Exhale gently before each swing. You see this done in all sports; in basketball by the free-thrower, in football by the punter, in baseball by the pitcher. It makes just as much sense to do it in tennis, especially when you're serving or receiving the serve.

When you feel yourself start to tighten up, that's probably exactly what is happening: your muscles (including the antagonists) are beginning to contract. Simply by exhaling and holding it for a count or two you can relax most of the muscles in your neck, chest, and shoulder regions. Then as the ball is put in play, raise muscle tension to whatever amount you consider necessary for the task at hand.

Control your breathing to relax between points too. You have thirty seconds to be ready to play between points and ninety seconds on the odd-game change-overs. Use as much of that time as you need to relax. Walk slowly to retrieve balls and breathe slowly and deeply as you do. While sitting at courtside during the change-over, systematically make all the large muscles in your body relax. Put your hands in your lap and let your shoulders droop, relaxing your neck and shoulder muscles. Then feel what's happening at your midsection, in your stomach, and at your lower back. Next, let that feeling of ease and comfort extend down to your legs and your feet. Finally, bend over at the waist with your arms hanging limply at your sides and let your entire body relax. Shake your arms and hands a bit to make sure they're as loose as you want them to be.

If you're a serious tournament player, it will be to your advantage to practice this relaxation routine separately. Use a clock to time yourself, to get accustomed to the time allotted (ninety seconds) so you'll not defeat your purpose by hurrying through the rest period. I've done it myself so I know you can learn to use most of that change-over time to good advantage. But this, too, is a learning process. It takes practice.

Discussing this matter of time between points and its effect on players, I'm reminded of an unusual and interesting incident involving world-class players. In the finals of a professional tournament Sandy Mayer, then ranked among the top twenty players in the world, was playing Jiri Hrebec, the Czeck player who was ranked far lower.

(A)   (B)   (C)

(D)   (E)

On this well-played backhand, the player bent her knees and straightened her arm to lower her racket to the low ball. By making these adjustments she was able to maintain her best wrist angle, the angle between her hand and her racket handle. She was able to avoid the weaker arched-wrist position.

Sandy won the first set and led in the second. Gradually and slowly, however, Hrebec began to close the gap. Eventually, he won both the second and third sets to close out the match.

Now those of us watching the match noticed a marked change of pace in it after the first set. Very simply, Hrebec delayed as much as permissible between points, toweling off, talking to spectators, discussing points with line judges and the umpire. It soon became apparent that he was controlling the time flow of the match. It became equally apparent that Sandy wanted to play at a faster pace. As we learned later, the slow pace induced by Hrebec upset Sandy and affected his game. When asked by reporters afterward how he explained the turn-around in his play and in the score, he replied, "Aw, I lost my rhythm." In response to reporters' questions of why the match changed so much after the first set, Hrebec said, "I broke his rhythm."

In that match, along with his rhythm, Sandy lost his "cool." He let Hrebec's antics disturb him, obviously. It was plain to see that he was agitated, that he became nervous and edgy over the many delays between points. To many of us watching, it was surprising that a player of his stature would let himself become upset that way. Sandy didn't like the between-the-points rhythm imposed by his opponent. But, in this case, about all he could do was adjust to it. When he didn't, his strokes suffered and his judgment in tactics and strategy suffered, too. Clearly, Hrebec won this battle of temperament. Sandy didn't stay relaxed.

You have the same opportunity and privilege to find your best pace and to play at it. You don't have to conform to your opponent's pace, as long as you stay within what the rules allow. If things are going badly for you, slow the pace. You can't call a time-out as is permitted in other sports, but you can manage to give yourself time to compose yourself, to figure out what's happening and to plan different strategy.

But if things are going well for you, play as fast as you can manage (unless, of course, that new pace begins to disrupt you). Get into position quickly after a point, walk quickly to retrieve balls, serve as soon as your opponent is ready. Play within the rules but try to rush your opponent so that he or she doesn't have time to analyze why he or she is losing. I've said it earlier and I say it here again. A tennis match is often a battle of temperament as well as a battle of strokes and tactics.

IMAGERY CAN HELP

You may find it easier to reduce mental tension through mental imagery rather than through muscle relaxation techniques. For years we in physical education have been advising our students to visualize their performance and the hoped-for result in both practice and play.

This was done in response to the increasing amount of evidence from laboratory experiments that indicates imagining helps. Now with the increased emphasis on psychology in sport, imagery is used in many sports by players at all levels of ability.

One good example of its use at top-level play comes from Jack Nicklaus who writes in his book *Golf My Way,* "First, I 'see' the ball where I want it to finish, nice and white and sitting up high on the bright green grass. Then I 'see' the ball going there; its path and trajectory, and even its behavior on landing. The next scene shows me making the kind of swing that will turn the previous images into reality."

Recall that this is similar to my earlier suggestion that you imagine the ball leaving a trailer of smoke as it leaves your racket. You thus "see" the flight and landing point of your shot just as Nicklaus "sees" his shot land.

The last part of Nicklaus' statement is important. *After* imagining the results of his shot he imagines himself swinging to make it. In tennis this can easily be done when serving. After you visualize the streamer of smoke, after you see the ball going over and in as you want it to, "see" yourself make the swing. In your mind's eye, see yourself make the throwing motion that is characteristic of good servers. For this you need not be very attentive to any one particular part of the swing. Rather, visualize the complete swing unless it's too complicated for you to do so.

While watching a nationally televised track meet, I saw a perfect example of this kind of mental imagery. Dwight Stones, the Olympic high jumper, used it in every one of his pre-jump routines. As he awaited his turn he went into a trance-like state, during which he obviously rehearsed his next jump. Viewers were able to see him bob his head as he imagined each step in his up-coming approach run. We conclude that he was mentally running, jumping, and clearing the bar.

You see most good servers do a similar thing after they take their position at the baseline. They look over the racket toward the net and into the service court, "seeing" the shot in their minds' eye, "seeing" the ball clear the net and land at their aim point. If you admit you feel nervous as you prepare to serve, try this kind of mental practice. It can help reduce tension.

In your imagination, see your shot go over and in as you planned. Then after that image is set in your mind, see yourself making the swing, as Nicklaus says he does. With this kind of mental activity, your mind will be too busy to worry about missing. With such a busy mind the typical self-critical and self-condemning thoughts that cause anxiety are dispelled. As a result, you're likely to be more confident.

And with that confidence, you're more likely to play up to your potential.

For this, find cues that cover more of the total action of a stroke or shot than do some of the others I mentioned earlier. As an example from another sport, my golf pro tells me that Sam Snead, the long-time great golfer, thinks of the word "oily" to remind himself how he wants his swing to feel.

When serving in tennis you might think of "throwing" your racket at the ball. Or "whipping it" through the serving motion may be more meaningful to you. You see that all of these cues evoke vivid images of the rhythm, the cadence, and the synchronization of the links of the kinetic chain involved in the serve. And again I say, when your mind is fully occupied with reproducing the swing patterns brought to mind by these cues, you're less likely to be overconcerned with the consequences of the result. To say it differently, you're less likely to be tense while making your swing.

From what my students tell me, I conclude that another likely place for tension to creep into your nervous system is when returning a serve on crucial points. If you're like the average inexperienced player, you probably often hope for a double fault instead of hoping for the chance to make a good return. This latter mental state alone may help you return better. But for another anti-choke device, one that puts your mind on something other than the fear of missing, try this.

Watch the server's ball-toss and try to notice whether the ball is spinning after the release. The instant you recognize that it is or isn't, tell yourself so softly. Say "yes" or "no," or "spin" or "no spin." It's really not important to you that your opponent does or does not spin it. But by playing that little game with yourself you'll be watching the ball come off the racket as you should. But even more important— you'll be less likely to freeze up. Your mind will be too busy to permit negative feelings to affect you.

Another device to use when receiving the serve is one you've probably noticed but not understood before. Jog in place for the moment or two before the server begins to serve. With that kind of movement you'll be making yourself loose physically, a condition that may keep you from tightening up mentally.

But for a more unusual and amusing example of imagery to reduce tension when returning the serve I turn to the field of American literature. While trying to help a male student learn to relax in this situation, I suggested he let his arms hang limply and that he bend and relax at the knees and at his waist. "Be loose, be limber!" I said. " Let your elbows and knees move back and forth and left and right; be loose jointed, not tense and muscular. Let your limbs move every which way as if you can't control them."

"Ah," he said, "you mean like Ichabod Crane." You probably know that he was referring to the pitiful school teacher in Washington Irving's classic tale, *The Legend of Sleepy Hollow.*

That incident occurred years ago. But when I reminded that student of it recently, to explain that I intended to relate it here in this book, his reply was noteworthy. " You can kid about it if you like," he said, "but that idea (image) still helps. I make myself feel like the sad, skinny guy from Sleepy Hollow. It helps me stay loose."

One of the most frequent occasions to choke during play occurs when you have to hit a passing shot against a net player. There's a certain finality about such a situation; either you finish the point with a winner or your opponent does with a volley. The crucialness of this situation causes many players to tighten up. As a result we see many bad misses, either in the form of mis-hits on the racket frame or as "out" or netted balls missed by a large margin. I know from my experience with students who make these errors that tension affects them. If it affects you too in these situations, try this anti-choke device.

Pretend you're merely engaging in target practice as you should often do in practice. This assumes, of course, that you've practiced passing shots in that frame of mind: trying to hit a target (the short corner or some other location within a few feet of a sideline). But the concept of target practice will help only if you've actually learned to make the shots in practice. If you practice long enough and often enough, you should learn to, provided you apply sound stroking technique. Recall again the free-throw shooter who won the game with two crucial throws. He knew he could make them because he usually made them in practice. In your crucial match situation, pretend you're back in a normal practice situation where you hit the targets time after time. Pretending this way is not easy to do. But it, like a physical skill, can be learned with practice. Especially if you practice under pressure as I've already described.

I've seen many players use evocative cues successfully on all strokes of the game. One of my male students hits a good backhand even under pressure by thinking of "giving the ball a karate chop," as he puts it. He bends his arm at the end of his backswing, then straightens it as he makes his forward swing. With that in mind, he's not concerned with body action, shoulder rotation or weight transfer. This may appear to be a serious omission on his part that could lead to disastrous results. But it doesn't. Those important movements seem to occur naturally as he "makes a karate chop." Luckily for him (and for me) I've learned not to disrupt his imagery for the sake of developing a better-looking stroke. He says his karate chop concept makes the backhand seem easy. You'll agree surely that this kind of confidence is an important step in developing a good backhand. And so I continue to encourage him to give the ball the karate treatment.

In contrast to that concept, a woman student of mine thinks of stroking her dog as she makes a backhand. I suggested that to her early in her training to correct a short, pokey motion she was making. I pointed out that the word "stroke" implies a long, smooth motion. I explained further that the shot is called a "stroke," not a poke and we both mimicked the motion used when stroking a dog. I pointed out that her hand is placed similarly, palm down, for both motions. She changed to the longer stroke pattern almost immediately. And she says she continues to recall that image when playing under pressure. She believes it helps her suppress the tension she would otherwise feel. It keeps her from poking at the ball as she used to do. But more important, it keeps her mind off the fear of missing.

Earlier I described how you can learn to run softly to steady your head when moving to reach a ball. I suggested you think of running on thin ice that could break under your weight. But a woman student of mine, a California native who has never seen thin ice on a lake or a pond, prefers her own cue. She imagines she's running along a sandy beach (these she has seen a lot of), full of sharp, jagged pebbles. So she sets her feet down softly to minimize the discomfort. On the court, it helps her keep her head steady as she strokes.

Bending the knees to get down to low balls should be a simple matter. It isn't always so, however. And strangely enough, it was a problem for a very athletic woman student of mine who excelled in track. I was able to induce her to bend properly, i.e., by lifting the heel of the foot that is farther from the ball, only after I showed her the similarity between that posture and her posture when she was "on the mark" to start a race. There, both heels are off the ground while the sole of each foot is pressed against the starting blocks. She tells me she still recalls that image during serious play and she feels it helps her avoid the straight-legged, droopy-wrist swing she used to make. She also explains that it has added new confidence in her backhand which goes in more consistently, probably because of better mechanics, but also because of less mental tension.

One last example of how imagery can help you suppress tension should suffice. This applies to one of the most difficult shots in the game: the half-volley.

One of my male students says he learned to relax when hitting his shot when I used the word "nudging" with him. As I watch him play the shot, he appears to be doing just that, just barely tapping the ball to nudge it on its way. He explains that this image keeps him from stroking too vigorously (the most common fault on half-volleys), from being too wristy, and from playing the shot carelessly.

I could give any number of these kinds of image-provoking words or concepts for you to use to reduce tension during play. Try these. But also search for others. As I said earlier, the best way to find them is to analyze what your shots feel like when you're playing well. Try to describe the feel of your swing to yourself, in your own words. There's a good chance that some of those words can become the cues you need to play with less tension.

SUMMARY. You can control your arousal level to bring it to an optimal point. First determine your best mental state. You may play best aroused. Or you may need to calm yourself down for best play. Some of the same cues you used in practice can be useful for controlling your anxiety level.

CHAPTER 9

PRACTICE (PROPERLY) TO MAKE PERFECT

OOOOOOOOOOOOOOOOOOOOOOOOOOOOOOOOO

As I said earlier, your aim in your pre-match routine should be to create a confident attitude toward the match. Confidence reduces anxiety and as a result, you'll have less interference due to muscle tension.

But how do we define confidence? And how can you develop it?

Confidence is a belief or a feeling that you can do a certain thing, such as make a passing shot, hit an overhead or serve deep to the backhand on a crucial second serve. But your belief must be based on fact, not merely on wishful thinking. To say it plainly, you have to know from previous experience, even if only from practice, that you have the capability to make the shot. Recall the basketball shooter I described earlier. He felt he could make the crucial free throws because he had made hundreds of them in practice. With that attitude there was no room for doubt and uncertainty to creep into his mind.

Having a confident attitude is a matter of training your mind. Many sports psychologists believe the reason for much of the success of the Russian Olympic performers is their mind-development programs. In their training, they place a great deal of importance on the mental approach to competition. They believe the mind determines the degree of success, since most Olympic competitors have the ultimate amount of physical skill.

In their mind-training programs, the Soviets learn to mentally erase the fear of failure and to mentally picture only successful performances. In addition, they teach their minds to "command" the body so that the skill of the body (attained through countless hours of practice) is available in competition. But they don't simply tell their mind what they want. They tell it that what they want they already have. In other words, the skill they learned in practice.

This concept that the mind can be used to control physical activity may appear to resemble inner-game theory. But notice the importance I—and the Russians—place on practice, a part of training very much neglected in inner-game theory.

In order to apply this kind of mind-ordering performance in tennis you must first learn to make the shot under stress-less conditions. Once suitable technique is developed, continue to practice it under stressful conditions.

You can create stress for yourself in practice by setting goals or objectives for your performance. When practicing serving, for example, set a target-number for successive good shots. See how many spin serves you can place deep in the backhand corner. How many cannonballs can you make when serving alternately from the right and left sides? Serve as many hard, first serves as you would in a match (twenty-four: six per game and four service games per set) and

This server's swing thought was "make a back-scratching loop with the racket." One way to learn to use such points of form in match pressure is to practice them in self-induced pressure drills. For example, try to make ten consecutive good serves to the backhand corner of the service court, or five to the left corner then five to the right, etc.

calculate the percentage. It may help if you record the scores and refer to them regularly so that you can compete against yourself.

I'm implying, of course, that in this kind of practice you'll be applying what you know about mechanics, aerodynamics and psychology to improve your strokes and to learn to make the shots. It's here, in this kind of pressure practice, that you learn what you can do and what you don't do well. With this knowledge, in the match play that follows, your intention should be to use more of what you can do and to avoid as much as possible what you can't do. In the pressure situations of match play, use only the shots you have confidence in, those that you make frequently in pressure practice. To say it differently, it's only by knowing you can do it because you've done it in practice that you can perform confidently in play.

PLAYING IS NOT PRACTICING

In tennis, as in other sports, merely playing the game may not provide sufficient practice in the many separate parts needed to play it well. For example, in an entire match, you may have only three or four chances to hit an overhead smash. That's hardly enough to enable you to learn to smash well. If you're like most players, you need to repeat a shot time and time again, over and over again—in practice— to be able, eventually, to use it properly in play. This, after all, is what learning is all about: developing habits so that actions are performed automatically and properly when there is no time for thought on these actions.

I learned many years ago that learning to play well takes time. Not just the passage of time, but time on the court. I know from personal experience as a player, a coach and a teacher that most good players are also good practicers. Most of them like to practice, either because they enjoy expending the effort and energy it requires, or because they realize how necessary it is if they are to reach their goals in the game.

Yet we occasionally hear of a skilled player who appears to minimize the importance of practice. For example, some good players claim to be able to play "in the zone," a psychological state in which good strokes and good shots are supposed to occur automatically, without conscious thought. I don't deny that many good players do feel that ability at one time or another. But neither do I overlook the many hours of practice they needed to learn the strokes they were able to produce automatically while playing in the zone.

Some players use an expression that conveys a more vivid image of their mental state during play. They say they sometimes feel as if they're playing "on automatic pilot," using the analogy of airplane flight. Here, too, good strokes and good shots are supposed to emerge automatically.

Tim Mayotte is shown returning a serve with a backhand slice. His location (on the baseline) indicates that he probably played the ball on the rise and that he chose to "pull" the ball down to prevent it from deflecting upward off his racket. On this kind of shot, the amount of spin applied to the ball depends on how sharply the racket is made to move downward from the plane in which it faces. Here Mayotte barely swung downward to apply only a minimum amount of spin.

But I find this expression equally misleading. As a former naval aviator, I know that it takes hours of practice at learning to set the controls properly—it's called "trimming the plane"—before a pilot gains confidence to trust the automatic pilot to direct the plane unerringly to its destination.

And so it is in tennis. I contend that players who attribute their success to their ability to play "in the zone" or on "automatic pilot" overlook the importance of practice. They've probably forgotten the countless hours they've spent working on their games either in lessons or with a rally partner or against a backboard or a ball-throwing machine. But work they did, and usually with a great deal of physical and mental effort. Only after reaching a certain level of development, the second level of those I described earlier, were they sometimes able to perform in the subconscious states they describe.

I saw a classic example of this during the last World Team Tennis season. Watching an inter-city match, I saw Sandy Mayer beat the

FOREHAND VOLLEY: The ball's flight off the racket is governed chiefly by where the racket faces and slightly by the direction in which it is moving. If they are not the same, the ball will go more toward the former. Here, the volleyer adjusts his wrist position to make his racket face to his left. The result is a crosscourt volley to his left. Reflex adjustments such as this are best learned in practice designed specifically for this purpose.

great Rod Laver 6-0 (in WTT a match consisted of just one set). It was apparent that Laver was trying his best but he couldn't do much against the "hot" Mayer.

Sandy tried to explain his exceptional play after the match by saying, "Everything just went right; every close call, every net cord shot went my way." Laver simply said, "I can't explain it."

There's no way of knowing precisely what Sandy was thinking of during the match. But we do know what he did in prepration for it: he practiced hard and long.

Prior to the match he had been in a slump and he had won far fewer matches than he was expected to. Luckily, a break in the league schedule gave him time to work on his game with his team coach, Frew McMillan, and together they sharpened Sandy's game. As a result his strokes and shots functioned perfectly. I contend that his practice, his work on his strokes, is what led to his good play in the match that followed. Whether he detached his mind from the match and simply went through the motions as if on automatic pilot is doubtful.

Like Sandy, you too will need to spend a great deal of time building your strokes or tuning them, and learning to use them in play-for-practice. Until you do, you'll be foolish to expect to be able to stroke automatically and unerringly in some kind of magical, mystical mental state. Neither are you likely to be able to rely on an automatic pilot. In other words, you'll not play well until you practice and learn to play well.

LEARN HOW TO PREPARE

If you're a serious tournament player (or even only a social club team player) develop a consistent pre-match routine. Start a few days before the match if possible. Find out how you, personally, best prepare for a match. What makes you really ready to play? How much of what kind of practice? And with whom?

I learned the value of this years ago when I was coaching top-flight collegiate players. I noticed that most of them asked for specific practice partners and for certain drills before important matches. When I became aware of preferences, I began to plan for them. Over the ensuing years, I let my players arrange their own pre-match practice routines, believing that players are more likely to feel confident and well prepared for a match if they practice what they feel they need.

To explain these differences, I recall that one player wanted to play someone he could beat easily. He needed this kind of assurance to face his next opponent confidently. But another of my players wanted to practice *and play* against a teammate who was better than he was. He explained that he'd feel more confident against an opponent who is weaker than his own practice partner.

Still on this point of personal preferences, some players wanted only to rally with steady teammates to solidify their strokes and to find their rhythms. Still others wanted a little of everything, some lobs, some smashes, some volleys, etc. They explained that they wanted to "touch up," to fine tune and to hone, all the strokes they were likely to use in the upcoming match.

Now, with these differences, I'm not suggesting that one is better for you than another. I'm merely suggesting that you learn how you personally best prepare for a match and that you arrange to prepare that way whenever possible.

PRACTICE AS OFTEN AS YOU CAN

Naturally, you're wondering how much time you should spend in practice. The answer depends on several things, not the least of which is your level of aspiration. How much to practice depends on how good you want to be, and on how badly you want to be that good. To state this last point differently, you must determine your degree of commitment and should allot your time on the court accordingly.

For the very serious-minded player, in any sport, no amount of practice is enough. If you haven't seen top-flight college teams or professional teams practice, and if you haven't seen young tennis players come up through the ranks, you'll be surprised to learn how hard they work at what appears to be done so easily in games. When you remember that most world-class players have been playing since childhood, you can imagine how many balls they've hit to perform as they now do.

Of course, you probably don't have the time, the energy, the ability, or the commitment to reach such a high level of skill. Still, the more practice you do, the better you're likely to play, provided you practice the right things and practice them properly.

There are right and wrong ways to practice. And there are do's and don't's for practice. For the remainder of this chapter I'll describe several of them while also listing several other important things for you to consider as you plan your practice.

In keeping with my emphasis on the concept of individual differences, I point out that players vary in the rates at which they learn skills in sport. At any new tennis skill—a backhand slice, for example— you may learn faster or slower than another person in your group.

If you're slower, don't be discouraged. Research findings in motor learning studies indicate that we can't predict eventual levels of attainment from rates of initial progress. You may eventually, by practicing harder and longer, develop a better backhand slice than some fast learners.

If you're a slow learner in tennis, you may avoid discouragement by understanding and accepting why you're slow. Possibly you've had less previous experience and so have fewer related moves to transfer to tennis. And if you're less experienced in tennis, you may not understand the goal or the purpose of certain court activities.

If you decide this is so, ask for help from a more experienced player. Do you know why you'd sometimes want to slice your backhand? Do you know specifically how the slice stroke differs from your previously learned drive stroke? Often, gaining insights like these enables slow learners to improve suddenly while still working on the same drill or practice routine.

Fast learners may have problems too. Often, quick, early progress is followed by long periods during which progress comes much slower. And with these come discouragement and less practice. And even less improvement.

You may be able to alter this chain of events by taking one positive step: practicing harder and longer.

Let's say, for example, you're working on a spin serve that you hope to eventually be able to bounce high to your opponent's backhands. You may have learned some first things about this serve quickly and thought you'd have no difficulty mastering it. But after some quick improvement, you found your progress slowed down and your practice no longer seemed to be paying off.

If you're in this kind of situation, don't be discouraged. Accept this as one of the conditions of learning. Naturally your progress will slow down as you try to refine your initial crude though successful attempts at serving. It may also slow down because you have less to learn about serving, and because what is left to learn must be done precisely. But if you're willing to put in the extra effort required, you may well develop a formidable spin serve.

PRACTICE CONTROLLING THE VARIABLES

Now let's consider some matters of practice that affect your ground strokes.

You will recall my opinion that play and practice are done differently at different levels of development. Learners building strokes spend most of their time rallying for that purpose. But other players who already have suitable stroke patterns are ready for more sophisticated practice. Before describing this kind of practice, let me refer back to a point of mechanics mentioned in my chapter on that topic.

Experience shows that despite the several forces acting on the ball at impact and immediately afterward, the direction of the ball's flight off your racket is governed jointly by where your racket is facing and the direction in which it is moving. You can improve your accuracy by practicing specifically to learn to control these two variables each time you swing.

You can increase your accuracy by practicing specifically to learn to control those two variables accurately each time you swing.

One way to do this is to hit several shots from a fixed location, the center mark, for example, while aiming at a target placed four or five feet inside the opposite baseline. After you develop reasonable skill at this, hit from various locations in your court while aiming at the same target. And finally, aim at targets placed at various locations while hitting from several different places in your court.

With this kind of practice you'll be making your strokes functional. You'll learn to recognize the changing conditions of play: your distance from the net and from your targets. And you'll learn to adjust the force of each swing and to select the proper trajectory of each shot. But most importantly, you'll learn to adjust your racket setting and the plane of your swing to each new situation. Experienced players react and adjust to these changing conditions of play almost subconsciously. But this ability may not come to you until after much practice and experience.

There undoubtedly are several other strokes or shots you should practice to raise your level of play. Decide what you need most and what is convenient to practice. Then arrange somehow to do it.

For example, let's say your serve is weak and your opponents don't seem to have much trouble returning it. Find other players of similar ability and explain your problem. Offer to serve to them while they practice making returns. You may have to emphasize that they'll be practicing too. Tell them you'll give them what they want: serves to the backhand, flat serves, spin serves. You may even agree to go to the net (to volley their returns) so they can practice passing shots. Or you may agree to stay back after serving so they can practice making deep returns. I know that many players who never before considered this kind of practice are pleased to do it.

For added benefit from this kind of practice, play imaginary games. Pretend you're trying to beat your practice partners by serving better than they can return. Ask them to aim at designated segments of the court and try to serve well enough to prevent them from hitting their aim points. Score a point in your favor each time they "miss." Score one for them each time they hit reasonably close to the target or you serve a fault.

If you need passing shot practice, find players who like to volley, or who need volley practice. Get their permission to pass them after giving them three or four consecutive volleys in each rally. Play imaginary games here too, counting your placements and errors. And keep score, too, to put some pressure on yourself.

To develop backcourt steadiness, find players who like to rally, who enjoy merely keeping the ball in play. As you rally with them, try to win each rally by outsteadying them. Count the number of successive good shots you make, and try to improve your score regularly. Putting pressure on yourself this way is one way of learning to be comfortable under pressure during serious play.

To get most value from your practice time, work on some specific point of form or of tactics. For this, consider the five basic play situations that occur during a match.

At any point in match play, you're in one of these situations: (1) You're serving. (2) You're receiving the serve. (3) You're rallying from the backcourt. (4) You're going to the net; and (5) You're playing against a net player. A few moments' thought should convince you

RETURN-OF-SERVE PRACTICE: The author is shown serving to a student to provide return-of-serve practice. The student, out of range in the foreground, tries to return deep to the backhand corner, aiming at the base of the target board set on the court as shown. A cord strung along the net and above it is set at the proper height for the deep shot intended. The student aims at the cord and the target board and learns to associate the two as he plans his return.

that these are essential parts of the game to practice. Spend most of your time on them.

But in addition there are several special things you should also work on. Drop shots, lobs and smashes, reflex volleying, varieties of spin, changes in pace, footwork, shot patterns—these are more or less important, depending on your style of play. Decide how much time to spend on each of them. Then work on them either separately, specifically, or as part of your play-situation practice.

One of the least practiced shots in the game is also one of the most important. I'm referring to the return of serve. Most average players make the mistake of ignoring it completely in their practice schedules, hoping to improve it during their match play. But consider this:

The average set consists of nine games, and the average game consists of six points. And so, in a 6-3 set, your opponent will serve four or five games, serving an average of ten or twelve times each game. You see, you'll be having to return about fifty serves in the total time it takes to play a set, about half an hour.

But in specific practice, you could have a partner serve about three times that number in half the amount of time. Obviously, this fifteen minutes can be better practice for you than the longer set. Of course, you should play-for practice too, even at the cost of time. You'll agree that I've already said so several times in this book.

SPACE YOUR PRACTICES PROPERLY

Maybe you feel you do practice enough to be a better player but you don't seem to be improving as much as you should. If so, perhaps you should consider revising your practice routines, if necessary, to put them in accord with the following principle.

Distributed practice is generally better than massed practice For example, twenty minutes of serve practice (or of any other skill) performed over three days is usually more beneficial than an hour of practice condensed into one session. And better still, would be three practice sessions crowded into one day, each lasting twenty minutes, and spaced hours apart.

There is some difference of opinion about proper arrangement of practice sessions. But a lot of evidence shows that some form of spacing is usually best.

The reason seems to lie in what happens in the nervous system. Experienced players admit it, and laboratory experiments offer objective proof of it: after a certain period of time spent on practicing a specific shot, (a forehand crosscourt, for example) a kind of numbness sets in to both the brain and the muscular system. As a result, the performance, the swing, is inhibited and so is done less efficiently, less accurately and perhaps even improperly. We may even say the player becomes bored with the activity and may need the excitement of newness to be stimulated to proper practice. And secondly, players may lose sensitivity in their muscles because of too much tension, and so may begin to perform badly. I've seen this happen time and time again in my lessons. Often, when practice is discontinued and then resumed later, even during the same lesson, I see instant improvement even beyond the point at which the last practice session ended.

The time periods and intervals I've mentioned here are arbitrary. You may be able to apply yourself for longer periods. Experiment, keeping in mind that you are to stop practice when you begin to feel insensitive, whether mentally or physically, to what you're doing.

MAKE PRACTICE SPECIFIC

Perhaps the most important word that can be said about practice is that it should be specific. This means that you learn only what you practice. And it suggests how you should practice: seriously.

The word "specific" applied to practice means that you should do in your practice program exactly what it is you intend to do in your matches. A good example of misapplication of this principle comes from our present national craze of jogging. Undoubtedly jogging has certain beneficial effects on your health. But as for movement during a match, it doesn't do much for you. After all, you're not intending to jog to reach balls hit by your opponents. Instead, you're going to have to move quickly, starting and stopping quickly and changing direction quickly. The theory of specificity suggests that to improve in those movement you'd best spend a lot of time practicing them. Doing so is a simple matter.

Stand at the center-mark in the conventional ready posture and practice starting quickly and moving quickly toward either sideline. As you approach each line, bend down and touch the line with your racket. Quickly then, reverse direction and hurry back to the center-mark. Repeat this over and over again, changing direction at will to touch either the left or right sideline.

Next move up to the volley location and straddle the center service line. Now move sideways to stretch as far as you can to reach imaginary passing shots. Here, though, use conventional volley footwork, making cross-over steps with the foot that is farther from the ball. After each lunge sideward, return quickly to the center line and make another cross-over lunge, to either the same direction or toward the other sideline.

For a final realistic (and therefore beneficial) on-the-court exercise,

THE OVERHEAD SMASH: On this overhead smash, the hitter is shown skipping backwards to get into position under the ball. Realizing that the ball is almost out of reach, she jumps to meet it. In the last frame she has begun to return to the volley position. This kind of footwork and jumping and returning to the volley location, when done frequently and continuously, provides good conditioning, and is in keeping with the theory of specificity which holds that the best way to condition for tennis is to do—in the conditioning program—the kinds of things that tire you in a match. The movements shown here are extremely tiring.

start again at the volley location. Now move backward quickly as if to stretch for and to swing at a lob. Make your typical smash swing, then quickly return forward to your volley location. Once there, lunge sideways to intercept imaginary drives. Return to the center line and move back for another imaginary overhead smash.

Do this kind of practice as often as you can and for as long as your energy and time permits. If you do it to and slightly beyond the point of fatigue, you'll be gaining the added benefit of anaerobic conditioning, conditioning for the kind of exercise that tires you during a match. Jogging, during which you're able to constantly replenish oxygen as you run, doesn't provide this. To say it specifically, this kind of conditioning is better for your tennis because it conditions you in the same way you get tired during a match—from bending, stooping, squatting, starting, stopping and changing direction.

Stroke practice should be done similarly, with maximum effort and full concentration. If you want to become a steady baseliner, practice being steady. Find a teammate or a friend who will agree to remain in the backcourt and give you the opportunity to hit many balls successively.

The way to develop the patience and the steadiness needed for baseline play is to practice them. Put some pressure on yourself in practice by setting some arbitrary number of good shots as a target. Try to progressively increase the number of shots, the length of your rallies, so you begin to feel comfortable in even the longest ones. It's a matter of training. Use the cues I've described earlier to shape your strokes and to get your mind off the pressure, off the fear of missing.

When practicing for this purpose you may benefit from thinking more of the outcome of your shot, of your objective, than of the physical performance of your strokes. Now obviously, your objective is to hit the ball in the court. But you can't do that unless you first hit it over the net. This then—clearing the barrier—may be a suitable objective, a suitable plan for both practice and play.

To induce you to consider this seriously, I tell you now of some interesting and surprising statistics. A few years ago, Jimmy Connors and Guillermo Vilas, two backcourt specialists, met in the finals of the U.S. Open. Because of their styles of play and because of the court surface, the match was mainly a backcourt duel. A statistician who tabulated the shots of the match tells that only 2% of the errors made were made into the net. Think of that: only 2%! I hope you will agree there can be no better example of what one of your main objectives should be during baseline rallies: make your shots clear the net.

Having been a college coach at the highest level of competition, I know how hard dedicated players practice to strengthen their weaknesses. At that level of play, deficiencies like a weak backhand volley, or a weak second serve, or inability to hit crosscourt can be disastrous against opponents who are able to exploit those weaknesses. This is why we see players spénding hours, days, weeks, and even months practicing to improve specific parts of their games.

For example, George Toley, former U.S.C. coach and known for his ability to tune the games of his high-level players, amuses listeners by telling how he "taught" Raoul Ramirez to hit his top-spin backhand. As Toley tells it, he spent an hour or two on successive days explaining the mechanics of top-spin and providing a couple of hundred shots for Ramirez to experiment with. Satisfied that Ramirez knew what to do, Toley gave him a bucket full of balls with the advice to practice for a week.

To describe the results, let me put it in Toley's words. "Son-of-a-gun, I'd see that kid out there day after day, sometimes alone on the court, bouncing balls to himself and hitting backhands. He'd grab any practice partner he could and ask for backhands. In a week he came back to me with a top-spin shot, which is now one of his better shots." Of course, Ramirez received reinforcement and encouragement from his practice partners at intervals. But the important point of this incident is that Ramirez practiced specifically, and with conscious thought, to apply the points of form suggested by Toley.

If you're serious about your game, practice as Ramirez did, specifically. For example, if you're weak on passing shots, practice these separately. I said earlier, it is one of the most neglected areas of practice even among experienced players (though obviously, not by Ramirez who went on from his college days to become a world-class player).

For beneficial passing-shot practice, find a partner who will feed balls to you from a volleyer's location so you can practice specific shots. For example, first hit many forehands down the line to your friend's feet while he or she stands in that particular short corner. Then have your friend move over to the other short corner (at the other sideline) so you can hit crosscourt to his or her feet. Do the same for backhands hitting many down-the-line shots, and then many crosscourts. As you practice these shots, notice which you do best. Are you better down the line or crosscourt? Are you better with a topspin drive or a flat one? Or possibly with a slice? Knowing what you do best is important because in play you should use that particular shot much more often than a riskier one, and almost always on a crucial point. Using your head this way in practice is a necessary step toward becoming a thinking player during matches.

Spend a lot of time in play-for-practice too. There, try never to miss into the net, or never to hit short of your opponent's service line. Try never to hit into the alley when your opponent is at the net, and to get your racket on every shot when you are at the net. Goals like these can make your practice much more beneficial.

PRACTICE CONCENTRATION

You may have read of a remark made recently by Martina Navratilova after she won a hard-fought match. "I really used my head out there. My I.Q. must have been 165 today." Not very likely, we know, but that's not the point. The point is that she used her head, or as she put it, "I really concentrated." Which applies perfectly to this discussion of specificity in practice.

Concentration can be learned just as strokes and tactics are learned—through practice designed specifically for that purpose. But first let's define the word. To many tennis players "concentration" means simply watching the ball, especially if they've been influenced by inner-game theory. But it can properly mean other things too. To some athletes it means bearing down, trying harder, going all out. To others it means focusing on the game, the contest, while ignoring outside influences. For still others, it means consciously blocking out negative thoughts that might impair performance. Usually this is done by focusing on positive thoughts, things to do rather than things to avoid, and on mentally "seeing" successful performances.

To some superstars, this kind of concentration becomes a kind of hypnosis. For example, players tell us that when John Newcombe was serving at his best he would often appear to stare down the receiver, defying him to return the next serve. The players say it often looked as if Newcombe not only intended to, but even expected to serve an ace. Frequently he did. Obviously, with that frame of mind, Newcombe was not worrying about missing.

A similar example comes from golf again. Long-time superstar Arnie Palmer has said that when he was putting well he often felt he had the power to think the ball into the hole. Consider that for concentration. He had such a strong image, such a strong picture of himself doing what he had to do that he felt he could make it happen on the strength of his will. No worrying about negatives there.

Now there's no guarantee that Newcombe's and Palmer's kind of positive visualization makes their shots go in as they imagined. But we can be fairly certain that a fearful, negative mental state on each serve or putt would have a detrimental effect.

Though you may not be able to concentrate your way into serving aces (because you may not have the physical ability) you probably can develop your powers of concentration to apply them to whatever level of skill you do possess. Maybe you hope only to serve to your opponents' backhand. Or perhaps to merely avoid a double-fault, backhand or no.

I've already described, in a general sense, what to think about, to concentrate on, during a match. You should be thinking about the broad trend of the match and should be planning either to maintain conditions or to change them to your advantage.

But there's a more specific kind of concentration that should occur on every shot. Fortunately, this kind is easy to learn in the popular and common drill of target practice.

Find a practice partner and agree to rally ground strokes while aiming at targets as I described earlier (your racket covers or the can balls are packaged in are suitable for this). When you miss a target badly, make a correction on the succeeding shot. Adjust one or more of the variables that affect the direction of your shot. To set them accurately you must be aware of your location as you make each shot. If you are deep behind your baseline you must hit higher and harder than when you're inside the line. And you must set your wrist differently to make your racket face the target as you hit from various distances from your sidelines.

Now all of this implies that you'll be thinking of those matters as you hit. I stress that this is exactly what you should be thinking of: setting the variables properly for each shot and correcting the settings after a miss. The reason for this is simple enough—the stroke is not set automatically, magically or mystically. Instead, you are in command and you must set it.

I remind you again, however, that you need not think of several little details of your swing. Rather, your nervous system gives a general command to hit higher or lower, softer or harder or whatever. And your body, trained in practice, responds accordingly. With sufficient practice like this you should learn to use your mind similarly in play. Lest you think this kind of heavy thinking is unusual, let me point out that Bjorn Borg says he often has a headache after a long match from concentrating so much. If during your practice and your play you think as hard and as long as you should, you too should feel mental relief afterward just as Borg says he does.

An experience with a student in one of my school classes provides an example of another kind of concentration, one equally effective. He asked for my help during return-of-serve practice, explaining that he had trouble changing quickly from his forehand grip (which was his "waiting grip," too) to his backhand grip when the server served to that side. Unfortunately for him, the two grips were so dissimilar that he had to make a marked change from one to the other. As a result he was not always able to set his hand precisely as he intended when he had to make a quick change to his backhand grip. The slight misplacement of his hand was not evident to me or to other observers but the player felt it clearly and showed it to us each time it occurred. And those returns were almost always inaccurate. My first suggestion as a possible solution to this problem—to use a Continental grip, a no-change grip mid-way between his forehand and backhand grips— was quickly discarded, because he had already tried it. He found that it didn't provide the sensitivity he needed to set his racket properly as he swung. Rather than setting its face perpendicular to the ground, as he intended, he mistakely either closed it or opened it. As a result, he either netted many balls or hit them higher than he intended. Clearly, the no-change grip was not for him. And so we began to look for other solutions to his problem. I watched him make several returns, some good, some bad, then asked what he was thinking about as he made those returns. He replied that he tried not to think, that he tried to "stay loose," as he put it. Now, luckily for both him and me, my next suggestion produced surprising results. I simply suggested that he think about his backhand grip (even while his hand was set in a forehand grip) while he was in his waiting posture. I told him to be attentive to what he feels as he changes grips, to be aware of the pressure points in his hand, and to think only of setting his hand properly as he makes his backswing. I explained that a serve to his forehand would not be a problem: he already had the grip for that shot and so he could make his return from that side without conscious thought. And so he was free to think about his backhand grip. I then began to serve to him.

The results were amazing. He immediately began to hit accurately—low and short when he wanted to, and high and deep when that was his intention. But equally important for this discussion was his surprise that such a simple solution to his grip problem had not occurred to him. In his defense, however, I can say that he had mistakenly been led to believe that his mind should be free, "detached," he said, from the act of returning the serve. For him there was a better way. He concentrated on his problem, his backhand grip.

The important thing to remember about this incident is that the player learned to make his grip change in practice. In that practice he concentrated. And he made it specific to one particular task. Keep this example in mind as you plan your practice. Carefully planned thoughtful and specific practice is more beneficial than loose, careless thoughtless effort. Which prompts me to say again—it is in practice that you learn to become a thinking player.

SUMMARY. The secret to better play is good, hard practice. Make practice specific. Practice controlling the variables in your strokes in addition to building the "look" of your strokes. Practice passing shots and serves and returns. Practice concentration and practice under stressful conditions. Practice as often as possible. And think about your strokes and shots as you practice them.

CHAPTER 10

PLAN YOUR TACTICS AND STRATEGY

OOOOOOOOOOOOOOOOOOOOOOOOOOOOOOOOOOOO

In the preceding chapters I stressed the importance of controlling your mental states during both practice and play. I've stressed that you must apply a great deal of conscious thought during practice of your strokes so you can stroke without much conscious thought during play. But there's more to playing well than just hitting well, even when you're hitting while in the proper frame of mind. You must also know where to hit. And you must know where to stand, and where and how to move. Which is to say you must learn to use your head to create favorable play situations, and to react to unfavorable ones created by your opponent.

At any given moment in a match you're likely to find yourself in one of several different play situations, depending on your, and on your opponent's, tactics and strategy. In some situations, as when serving or receiving the serve, you have time to set yourself nicely into position. You may even be able to plan your next shot or two in advance. But once the ball is in play, the action may be too fast and the tactical situations too varied to allow you to follow a fixed game plan.

For example, you may find yourself in a backcourt rally in which you're sparring with your opponent, hoping to create an opening, planning to attack. But suddenly you see your opponent attacking, taking a short ball and charging to the net.

Tactical situations like these (rallying from the backcourt, going to the net, and defending against a net rusher) are likely to occur on any point after the serve and the return of serve are put in play. In each of these situations there will be a number of decisions for you to make and a number of options for you to choose from. I list many of them here and suggest that you begin now to consider which you can use effectively. This knowledge and these decisions are essential parts of any thinking player's game plan. Make them part of yours, too.

ADJUST YOUR SERVING TACTICS

Though most world-class players rely on their serves as offensive weapons, you need not serve as well as Tanner, Amaya, or Wade to win a majority of your service games. But you must avoid double faults. And you must serve with sufficient force and accuracy to prevent your opponent from attacking on the return. Planning your service strategy in advance will often help you serve effectively though your serve is not in itself a strong shot. One important decision to make is whether to run to the volleying location after your serve or to remain in the backcourt. Make this decision on the basis of your ability to serve and to volley. And, of course, on the basis of your opponent's ability to handle your serve and your volleys.

If you intend to remain in the backcourt after your serve, experi-

FOOTWORK DURING THE SERVE: When you apply force diagonally upward, you may leave the ground as a result of those forces. Here the server has crossed his rear foot (the right one) over the line and is about to land on it in front of the line. Meanwhile, his left foot is also off the ground. If you try to deliberately maintain contact with the ground, you'll not be using one of the most effective sources of force—upward thrust at the feet and knees.

ment to find the best location from which to serve. Sometimes stand next to the center mark and hit straight along the center line. Occasionally stand closer to the sideline and hit a sharply angled ball (as Ashe did to Connors at Wimbledon). Notice which procedure draws a weaker return or gives you an easier shot on your next stroke. Serve from that location a majority of the time. And aim most of your serves to the receiver's weak stroke. It's usually the backhand. Practice to develop this ability—to serve to your opponent's backhand anytime you want to and especially when serving under pressure on crucial points. But vary the placement of your serves enough to make the receiver uncertain about your intentions.

Still, there may be times when you'll be better off serving to create a weakness rather than serving to an opponent's built-in stroke weakness. For example, a wide serve to a strong forehand may force your opponent out of position and so give you an opening for your next shot. Consider the advantages and possibilities of each placement.

One popular maxim in the game states that a player is only as good as his or her second serve. As you consider this, let me remind you that even world-class players miss their first serve cannonballs about half the time. Surely then you and I will miss ours at least that often. Now if our second serves are weak enough to allow our opponents to attack with their returns, we're not serving effectively. The solution here is to hit first serves more carefully, perhaps by putting more spin on the ball (which means taking some of the speed off of it), even if it means giving up chances for aces. With more medium-paced first serves going in, opponents will have less opportunity to attack weak second serves.

If your opponent continues to attack your serves, be alert to the depth of them. Chances are they're landing short in the service court. If so, change the placement of your toss or your wrist position, to change the position of your racket on the ball. I discussed these adjustments earlier and related them to the fundamental fact of the game: the ball goes where your racket faces.

The kind of thinking required here to figure out what adjustments to make should keep you so busy you don't have time to think of the consequences of missing. So I say again, with your mind occupied this way, you'll be inhibiting the tension that often arises when you are concerned with the fear of missing.

After serving, place yourself midway between two imaginary lines drawn from the receiver's location to the widest possible aim points in your court. As you draw the imaginary lines, in your mind's eye see a third line midway between the two extending from the receiver's location, through or under the net, through your court and beyond your baseline. This line is known as both "the line that bisects" and "the line of good position." As those names suggest, it places you in the best location to reach shots hit to either side of you.

If your serve is aggressive and at least reasonably hard to handle, and if you volley reasonably well, you may wisely decide to run to the net immediately after your serve. If this is your plan, stand close to the center mark. From this location you'll be able to get reasonably close to the net, on the line that bisects, for your first volley. If you've served a cannon-ball, you'll have time for only two or three steps before having to make a split-stop to prepare to move to intercept the return. After a slower serve you'll have time for four or five steps. In the first instance, you'll be volleying from "no-man's-land," usually considered a risky procedure. But if your serve is fast enough and difficult to handle you may not be badly off volleying the hoped-for weak returns even from that dangerous location. Deciding whether to take such a calculated risk should become part of your thinking game. You may decide during your prematch planning to use this tactic, or you may discover during the match that this tactic is effective.

VARY YOUR SERVE RETURN TACTICS

Like the serve, the return of serve is one of the few situations where you'll have time to set yourself nicely into position and to plan your next shot or two in advance. But once the ball is served, you'll have to cope with a variety of speeds, spins, and angles. You'll also have to notice whether the server runs to the net or stays back.

If you're having trouble returning your opponent's serves, experiment to find the best place to stand. For a fast serve you may have to stand a step or so behind the baseline to have time enough to move and to swing. But from there, you'll have a wide angle to cover, so it may be to your advantage to stand on the baseline or even closer (provided you can move quickly enough) to reduce the distance you have to move to reach wide serves.

If your opponent has a high-bouncing spin serve, your best plan may be to play the ball as it rises. For this, a slice is often best. But if this proves too difficult, stand back farther to let the ball come down. From that deeper location you'll probably have time for a fuller swing. Try both methods to see which works best for you in each particular match.

If a net-rushing server shows that he or she can volley effectively after the serve, hit a majority of your returns crosscourt so that you'll not have to chase sharply angled volleys to an apparent opening. Crosscourts may lure the server into hitting parallel to the far sideline and so you'll not have to chase any wider than that line. But when you aim crosscourt, aim for the "short corner," where the service line intersects the sideline. A deep crosscourt is likely to be within reach of the server-volleyer.

But if the server stays in the backcourt after serving, try to return deep to the backhand corner. Such a shot will eliminate any advantage the server has by serving. Yet, if the serve forces you very wide in your court, your best play may be crosscourt to bring the line of good position, the line that bisects, closer to you. You may have to make this choice instantly as you see the placement of the serve.

If you intend to run forward to volley after your return, your best return is along the line unless the serve is very short (in which case you may hit to either corner of your opponent's court). If you make the server hit from close to that line, you'll have less distance to run to reach the line of good position for your opponent's next shot. As a result you're more likely to be able to volley aggressively on your first volley.

Unlike what occurs on other groundstrokes, play when returning serves is often so fast that you must decide your intention before hand. A good procedure is to use whatever shot you feel you make best; i.e., down-the-line or cross-court slice or drive. As the match progresses, try to notice which of those choices is working best for you. Use it a majority of the time and almost always on crucial points.

PLAY OFFENSE AND DEFENSE
FROM THE BACKCOURT

If you don't serve and volley well enough to win on the strength of those strokes, plan tactics and strategy around your backcourt game. Practice to develop the ability to control play from the baseline. But before trying to control rallies, practice to develop steadiness. Remember, the majority of points are won on errors, so cut down your groundstroke errors. Plan to keep the ball in play long enough to match your opponent's rallying ability, so you can wait for a safe opportunity to attack, even while you're hoping for an error on your opponent's part.

Your best location for most baseline play, is one step behind your center mark. But if your opponent is hitting from an alley, stand two or three feet to either side of the mark (away from your opponent) to be on the line that bisects the angle of the possible returns.

If you can control the depth of your shots, hit them deep enough to keep your opponent away from the net (unless you conclude that he or she is a weak volleyer in which case you may wisely hit short to lure him or her to the net). To control the depth, adjust the height of your shots. If you hit flat shots, and want more depth, you need only to aim higher. But if you hit with top-spin, you'll have to hit higher and harder to maintain that amount of spin and still hit deeper.

BACKHAND SLICE: Good form at the finish of a backhand slice. Here, the high rear shoulder and the correspondingly low front one indicate that this player swung her racket in a diagonally downward plane, from high to low. She has maintained her wrist angle, between her forearm and racket handle, and thus has not used much wrist motion. Instead, she appears to have used total arm action, the best way to control the force of her swing, the swing plane, and the racket angle.

The left-to-right direction of your shots is important too. Average players have weaker backhands than forehands. So hit most of your shots to that weaker stroke. Rally to it. Attack it. And hit to it for defensive purposes if possible. But as you consider the relative strength of your opponent's strokes, calculate the percentages of your opponent's hits and misses. He or she may be making more errors on a spectacular, hard-hit forehand than on an obviously softer backhand. If so, you may best purposely play to that strong—but erratic—forehand.

When you're relying on steady baseline play to win, you must maintain good position. A frequently overlooked point of tactics may help you in this respect.

When an opponent has you running toward a sideline and you feel you may have trouble getting into position for the next shot, hit crosscourt. If possible make that a high, floating shot rather than a crisp one. A crosscourt shot is likely to make it easier for you to reach the line of good position as your opponent makes his/her next shot because it brings that line closer to you. On the line of good position you'll be properly off-center and in best location to reach your opponent's shots to either your right or left.

A crosscourt shot offers a second advantage when you are out of position. It may lure your opponent into hitting parallel to the far sideline, to the apparent opening. Consequently, you'll not have to chase any wider than that sideline to reach the ball.

When playing in windy conditions you must be even more alert than on a calm day. Know every moment what the wind is doing. Be alert for sudden gusts and adjust your shots accordingly. When hitting with a strong wind, keep your shots low. When hitting against the wind, hit harder and higher to get the depth you want. Certain cross-wind conditions may give you a down-wind shot. You may be able to maneuver your opponent to get a chance to attack with that shot.

And lastly, when playing in the wind consider the drop-shot. The safest time to try such a shot is when you are hitting against the wind. If you drop shot when hitting with the wind, the force of the wind may cause the ball to "carry" toward your opponent both during its flight and after it bounces.

PLAN TO DEFEND AGAINST NET PLAY

A little-known statistic should help you combat an opponent's net rushing tactics. More points are lost on passing shot errors than are won on volleys, which suggests that you'll be wise to make your opponent show that he or she volleys well enough to beat you. In other words, keep the ball in play, somehow. Don't beat yourself by missing a large percentage of your attempts to pass. On very difficult-to-handle approach shots, your best shot for keeping the ball in play may be a lob.

When you attempt to pass a net player consider the angles open to you. If you are hitting down the line your shot may be either short or deep and still be out of the volleyer's reach. But if you decide to hit crosscourt you must hit to the short corner (where the service line meets the sideline) to place it out of reach of the net player. A deep shot is likely to be within his or her reach. These advantages of one option over another may help you decide which to try. If you don't have a good, reliable, short crosscourt shot your percentage shot may be down-the-line.

When hitting from close to a sideline, however, you may sometimes intend to continue the rally rather than to end it with a passing shot at that instant. If so, your best shot may be crosscourt to lure your opponent into hitting parallel to the far sideline. Again, you'll not have to run beyond that line, wider than it, to retrieve your opponent's volley.

This is the second instance in which I've suggested you hit a crosscourt shot when you are out of position. In both cases, when your opponent is in the backcourt and when he or she is at the net, crosscourts can help you get out of trouble and can keep you in the rally. This explains why good baseline players hit a majority of their shots crosscourt during rallies.

As I suggested earlier, you ought to use your best passing shot, the one you have most confidence in, much more often than an uncertain one. And almost always on crucial points.

When playing against a known net rusher, you can often take the sting out of his or her net game by keeping your rally shots deep. For this purpose, high soft shots of yours may be more effective than hard, low, short ones. Adjust the height of your shots at the net to attain the depth you want.

I've already mentioned a couple of popular maxims of the game ("You're only as good as your second serve," and "Crosscourts keep you in the rally"). A third one suggests that a lob may often be your best play against a net player. I'm referring to the expression, "A net game is only as good as that player's overhead smash." The implication here is that you'll do well to lob frequently against an opponent who doesn't have a strong, reliable overhead smash.

As I've suggested earlier, as a thinking player you should tabulate the results of your and your opponent's shot. Decide what's winning for you, or losing for you. If the match is going against you because of your opponent's aggressive net play, analyze your shots to determine if a change of tactics will help. Decide whether to lob more or to drive more, to risk harder passing shots or to play them more carefully. Or perhaps your best tactic may be to get to the net first,

(A)   (B)

(C)   (D)

(E)   (F)

The author is shown running to the net after an approach shot. The points to notice are the hop into the ready posture (as his opponent meets the ball); the cross-over step to reach the ball after only a momentary pause to determine its direction; the restricted backswing; and the wrist position, cocked and laid back, to place the racket properly behind the ball.

ahead of your opponent. Knowing what's happening and deciding what to do about changing a losing game is one mark of a thinking player.

PLAN YOUR NET ATTACK

Net play is one useful dimension to the game. But it isn't essential. Both Connors and Borg, and Evert and Austin, too, seldom go to the net. All of them prefer baseline play. But as I've said earlier, the more weapons you have to call on in time of need, the more effective you're likely to be.

Practice net play to see if you have the necessary qualities for it and to develop the strokes and shots that can be effective in it. In your play-for-practice, apply the teaching points I list here, in this last of the five basic play situations. These kinds of "heady" tactics alone may make you a better net player.

If your plan is to go to the net during a baseline rally, apply the same rules of percentages I mentioned earlier. Don't beat yourself by missing approach shots that you play too aggressively. Play your shots carefully enough to make a good percentage of them. Make your opponent show that he or she can pass well enough to beat you.

Go to the net only when hitting from inside your baseline so you can reach an aggressive volley location. This may require patience on your part, patience to wait for a short shot from your opponent.

Aim most of your approach shots to your opponent's weaker stroke. For nine out of ten players, it's the backhand. You'll probably benefit from hitting to a stronger forehand occasionally, however, to keep your opponent from protecting that weaker backhand.

If your opponent seems to be hitting most of his or her shots to the middle of your court (rather than angling shots close to the sidelines) it's probably because he or she can't hit angled shots accurately. This is true of many steady baseliners especially those known as "pushers" who seem simply to push every ball back to the center of their opponent's court. One way to force them to hit angled shots is by using a net-rushing center theory.

As the name implies, hit your approach shots to the center of your opponent's court and run forward to the volley location. From the center, your opponent will have to hit for the sidelines to put the ball out of your reach. These are the kind of angled shots he or she doesn't have or doesn't like.

The most effective way to apply the center theory is to first hit wide to your opponent's forehand and then to place the return down the center to his or her backhand. Few players can pass consistently from such a situation so be prepared for a lob. But at the same time be ready to move forward after your split-stop in case he or she does try to pass you.

At the same time that the center theory makes it difficult for an opponent to pass you, so does it make it more difficult for you to angle your volley away for a winner. Your centered approach shot places your opponent in midcourt, equidistant from each sideline. And so you must volley accurately and forcefully to win. You must appraise this situation carefully therefore. If you can volley better when your opponent is in midcourt than he or she can pass from that location, it may be to your advantage to use your net game this way—with the center theory.

I hope you'll agree that my listing of these tactical tips is a fitting way to end this discussion of tennis for the thinking player. But let me caution you that you shouldn't expect to ever become equally adept in all five basic play situations. Even world-class players aren't. Chris Evert, for example, is not a serve-and-volley specialist. She relies mainly on her groundstrokes. But Butch Walts' strength is in his serve. He relies mainly on that shot to at least stay even in a match. In other words, they both know their strong points and plan their strategy around them.

You, too, should know what you do well. You should know, or soon discover, what your opponent can't do well. And you should know how to use your strength against your opponent's weakness.

But all this presupposes that you've practiced the tactics and strategy you intend to use. You'll agree surely that I've stressed the importance of practice in this book. And I've stressed the importance of thinking during play. We can summarize this relationship between practice and play by saying, "in practice, plan your work; in a match, work your plan." To do so you'll have to become a thinking player, playing while you think.

SUMMARY. Apply conscious thought to determine your best tactics and strategy in each match. Practice the tactics you intend to use. Practice against the tactics your opponent is likely to use. Be ready with a list of options you may use in various play situations. During play, decide which options are working to your advantage. Play while you're thinking, as described in the first chapter.